How to access the supplemental web resource

We are pleased to provide access to a web resource that supplements your textbook, *Beginning Ballet*. This resource offers photos and video clips of ballet techniques, learning activities, assignments, quizzes, and much more.

Accessing the web resource is easy!
Follow these steps if you purchased a new book:

1. Visit **www.HumanKinetics.com/BeginningBallet**.

2. Click the <u>first edition</u> link next to the book cover.

3. Click the Sign In link on the left or top of the page. If you do not have an account with Human Kinetics, you will be prompted to create one.

4. If the online product you purchased does not appear in the Ancillary Items box on the left of the page, click the Enter Key Code option in that box. Enter the key code that is printed at the right, including all hyphens. Click the Submit button to unlock your online product.

5. After you have entered your key code the first time, you will never have to enter it again to access this product. Once unlocked, a link to your product will permanently appear in the menu on the left. For future visits, all you need to do is sign in to the textbook's website and follow the link that appears in the left menu!

→ Click the Need Help? button on the textbook's website if you need assistance along the way.

How to access the web resource if you purchased a used book:

You may purchase access to the web resource by visiting the text's website, **www.HumanKinetics.com/BeginningBallet**, or by calling the following:

800-747-4457 . . . . U.S. customers
800-465-7301 . . . . Canadian customers
+44 (0) 113 255 5665 . . . . European customers
08 8372 0999 . . . . Australian customers
0800 222 062 . . . . New Zealand customers
217-351-5076 . . . . International customers

For technical support, send an e-mail to:

support@hkusa.com . . . . U.S. and international customers
info@hkcanada.com . . . . Canadian customers
academic@hkeurope.com . . . . European customers
keycodesupport@hkaustralia.com . . . . .Australian and New Zealand customers

HUMAN KINETICS
The Information Leader in Physical Activity & Health

08–2013

This unique code allows you access to the web resource.

Access is provided if you have purchased a new book. Once submitted, the code may not be entered for any other user.

Product: Beginning Ballet web resource

Key code: KASSING-97ZU3D-OSG

Beginning Ballet

INTERACTIVE DANCE SERIES

Gayle Kassing, PhD

Human Kinetics

Library of Congress Cataloging-in-Publication Data

Kassing, Gayle.
Beginning ballet / Gayle Kassing.
    p. cm. -- (Interactive dance series)
  Includes bibliographical references and index.
  1. Ballet--Handbooks, manuals, etc. I. Title.
  GV1787.K285 2013
  792.8--dc23

                   2012022050

ISBN-10: 1-4504-0249-6 (print)
ISBN-13: 978-1-4504-0249-1 (print)

The web addresses cited in this text were current as of January 22, 2013, unless otherwise noted.

Acquisitions Editor: Scott Wikgren; **Developmental Editor:** Bethany J. Bentley; **Assistant Editor:** Derek Campbell; **Copyeditor:** Joanna Hatzopoulos Portman; **Indexer:** Sharon Duffy; **Permissions Manager:** Dalene Reeder; **Graphic Designer:** Joe Buck; **Graphic Artist:** Kathleen Boudreau-Fuoss; **Cover Designer:** Keith Blomberg; **Photographer (interior and cover):** Bernard Wolff, unless otherwise noted; photo on p. 138 © Jose Luis Villegas/Sacramento Bee/ZUMA Press; **Photo Asset Manager:** Laura Fitch; **Visual Production Assistant:** Joyce Brumfield; **Photo Production Manager:** Jason Allen; **Art Manager:** Kelly Hendren; **Associate Art Manager:** Alan L. Wilborn; **Illustrations:** © Human Kinetics; **Printer:** Versa Press

We thank Parkland Theatre in Champaign, Illinois, for assistance in providing the location for the photo shoot for this book. We also thank Twist and Shout Dance and Cheer in Mahomet, Illinois, for providing equipment for the photo shoot.

Printed in the United States of America   10 9 8 7 6 5 4 3 2

The paper in this book is certified under a sustainable forestry program.

Human Kinetics
Website: www.HumanKinetics.com

United States: Human Kinetics
P.O. Box 5076
Champaign, IL 61825-5076
800-747-4457
e-mail: humank@hkusa.com

Canada: Human Kinetics
475 Devonshire Road Unit 100
Windsor, ON N8Y 2L5
800-465-7301 (in Canada only)
e-mail: info@hkcanada.com

Europe: Human Kinetics
107 Bradford Road
Stanningley
Leeds LS28 6AT, United Kingdom
+44 (0) 113 255 5665
e-mail: hk@hkeurope.com

Australia: Human Kinetics
57A Price Avenue
Lower Mitcham, South Australia 5062
08 8372 0999
e-mail: info@hkaustralia.com

New Zealand: Human Kinetics
P.O. Box 80
Torrens Park, South Australia 5062
0800 222 062
e-mail: info@hknewzealand.com

E5318

Contents

8 History of Ballet 115

Preface

Ballet began as a source of amusement for royalty. Today it has evolved into a source of delight for children, an alternative form of training for athletes and performing artists, and a passion for millions of dancers and spectators. Ballet instruction for all ages and interest levels has proliferated through community dance studios and arts programs, professional training schools, and high school and higher education courses.

A beginning ballet class requires both physical and mental participation. In courses such as English literature or Western civilization, you sit in class, listen to the teacher, take notes, work on projects, read the text, prepare outside assignments for class, and take tests. In ballet class, the teacher presents a series of exercises and combinations, and then you execute them. Throughout the class, you mentally take notes to learn the sequence of movements that comprise an exercise or combination. The teacher gives feedback on how to sharpen or refine your performance, and you remember that feedback in order to apply it the next time you execute the movement.

In a single ballet class students practice a variety of exercises, steps, and combinations. Throughout a course, the number of exercises, steps, and combinations increases and they become more complicated and difficult. It is often a challenge to understand the elements and technique requirements of each exercise or step that is presented in only one part of a class. Beyond learning the sequence of movements of an exercise or step, you must recognize and execute it and all its parts, then connect it to its French name. Compounding this situation, you must comprehend how these exercises, positions, poses, steps, and combinations relate to each other as part of beginning ballet technique. To alleviate confusion, you need both written and visual resources to support learning ballet technique and about ballet as an art form.

Beginning Ballet is a comprehensive book for students enrolled in a high school or college beginning ballet course. It may be taught in a fine arts, physical education, or dance program as either a general education course or an introductory course for dance majors or minors. The book prepares you for participating mentally and physically in a beginning ballet class. It presents the fundamentals of ballet technique and movement principles, introduces barre exercises and center steps, and provides a concise history of ballet artists and significant ballets to support you as an audience member. Learning ballet and learning *about* ballet are the first steps in understanding and appreciating it as a form of movement and as a performing art.

Chapter 1 introduces you to ballet as an art form and to the structure of the ballet class. It covers the changing ballet traditions and how ballet has proliferated in community and academic settings that afford you options if you wish to continue your ballet studies. Chapter 2 prepares you for taking ballet class, selecting proper dance wear and shoes for class, understanding expectations of participants, and class etiquette. Chapter 3 addresses dance safety, basic anatomy, injury prevention, and awareness of proper nutrition and hydration. Chapter 4 explains basic foot and arm positions, classical body positions, and poses of ballet. Chapter 5 describes principles of movement in ballet, how music supports the dance, and structure and design of basic ballet exercises and combinations. It provides strategies for learning ballet technique and preparing for performance testing in class. Chapter 6 illustrates the exercises that you study at the barre. Chapter 7 explores beginning ballet steps learned in the center part of class. In chapters 6 and 7 sequential photos illustrate the key positions in each exercise. Chapter 8 gives a brief historical survey of ballet, focusing on prominent world contributors, styles, and works. The chapter provides strategies for viewing and reporting on ballet performances, which contribute to developing aesthetic values about ballet as a performing art.

The book contains a glossary of beginning ballet terminology, sidebars, and special elements such as self-check activities and historical tidbits to extend your ballet learning.

The web resource that accompanies this book offers supplemental, interactive instruction. Visit www.HumanKinetics.com/BeginningBallet1E to check it out. This resource provides you with added opportunities to practice the dance steps explained in this book.

When you participate in a ballet class, you join a tradition shared by all ballet dancers worldwide. Participating in beginning ballet can help you to

+ develop new movement and dance skills and strengths,
+ explore a performing art that started in the Renaissance and continues as a powerful dance form in the 21st century,
+ understand a dance form that supports other dance forms and performing arts, and
+ learn about yourself physically and mentally.

When you step into a ballet studio, you enter a unique world where you can learn to execute movements that have evolved over four centuries. In this world you can also learn about yourself through an intense mind–body discipline.

This book helps you take your first step into the world of ballet.

How to Use
the Web Resource

In a ballet class, exercises and combinations can move quickly. They can also contain many new movements or small additions to existing movements you have learned. However, you have an added advantage! Your personal tutor is just a few clicks away and is always available to help you remember and practice the exercises executed in class. You can study between class meetings or when you are doing mental practice to memorize exercises or steps. Check out the book's accompanying web resource at www.HumanKinetics.com/BeginningBallet1E.

The web resource is an interactive tool that you can use to enhance your understanding of beginning ballet technique, review what you studied in class, or prepare for performance testing. It includes information about each exercise, step, position, or pose, including notes for correct performance; photos of positions and poses; and video clips of exercises and steps. Also included are interactive quizzes for each chapter of your *Beginning Ballet* text, which let you test your knowledge of concepts, ballet basics, terminology, and more.

In a beginning ballet class, students learn about ballet technique, ballet as an art form, and themselves. The Supplementary Materials section of the web resource contains the following additional components for each chapter of your *Beginning Ballet* text. These components support both learning in the ballet class and exploring more about the world of ballet.

- Glossary terms from the text are presented so that you can check your knowledge of the translated meaning of the term as well as a description of the term.

- Web links give you a starting place to learn more about a ballet work, its style, or companies that present the work.

- Some chapters include e-journaling prompts and assignments to think more deeply about beginning ballet class.

- Other assignments include specific activities to apply the concepts and ideas about ballet.

We hope that the web resource helps you to individualize your learning experience so that you can connect to, expand, and apply your learning of beginning ballet, enhancing your success and enjoyment in your study of this dance form.

Chapter 1

Introduction to Ballet

Ballet dancers glide, spin, and leap across the floor. Like all artists, ballet dancers learn technique that they refine into artistry through continuous study. In the studio, dancers perfect ballet exercises, steps, and combinations that are the basis for choreography performed on stage. When you enter the dance studio to begin your studies, the studio becomes your portal into the world of ballet, as it has been for generations of dancers.

Ballet class is the starting point for learning ballet. Attending class is the training constant for all dancers, from beginners to professionals. The class is the force that drives the development of the dancer in technique and artistry to achieve better performance of the art.

Ballet is a Western classical dance form and a performing art that is over four centuries old. At the heart of ballet is its technique, which has evolved through contributions from dancers and choreographers worldwide. Over time, ballet has absorbed movement principles and developed various styles linked to historical periods, schools, and methods that support its aesthetics as a performing art.

Ballet technique comprises a vocabulary of exercises, steps, positions, and poses. A significant feature of ballet technique is the dancer's use of **turnout,** where the legs externally rotate from the hip sockets. Underlying this codified vocabulary of movement are principles and protocols for performing ballet. Thus, when you study ballet, you learn the language of this dance form. Knowing the vocabulary helps you to understand and communicate the many possibilities for combining exercises, steps, and poses into various combinations and pieces of choreography. Performing ballet technique requires precision, clarity, and coordination of the torso, legs, arms, and head. Several ballet schools and methods represent distinct styles for performing ballet technique.

> ## DID YOU KNOW?
>
> Many ballet works have been handed down from one generation of dancers, teachers, and choreographers to the next. Until the invention of film and later electronic recording, dancers, choreographers, and **regisseurs**, or individuals who stage a dance work, kept a visual memory bank of ballets they would restage for a ballet company. They could remember, dance, and teach entire ballets and all the different dancers' parts.

In addition to technique and vocabulary, dancers practice many traditions in ballet classes. These traditions contribute to making ballet a unique dance form. Both oral and written traditions provide a framework for etiquette and expectations in class and performance.

Ballet continues to develop while holding on to its romantic, classical, and 20th-century style dance works. In the 21st century, ballet has expanded beyond a dance and performing art form; it is also used as physical training for professional athletes and as an alternative workout routine for fitness enthusiasts. The world-famous New York City Ballet published a ballet fitness workout. Other dance forms use ballet as part of their training.

BENEFITS OF STUDYING BALLET

Some people see a ballet performance and they are so dazzled by the beauty and grace of the dancers that they want to learn how to perform ballet. Studying ballet as a young adult can be a new adventure or a reconnection to previous study. Some people take a beginning ballet class to extend their studies and support another form of dance, art, or other study. Often drama, music, or musical theater students take ballet to expand their movement abilities. Likewise, athletes such as gymnasts, skaters, basketball players, and football players enroll in ballet to increase their strength, agility, and balance. Ballet has countless benefits for everyone, including the following:

- It helps improve posture and coordination.
- It increases physical activity, which supports weight control and general fitness.
- It increases flexibility, strength, and balance.

- It promotes poise and graceful, creative movement.
- It simultaneously stimulates mental and physical engagement, providing an enjoyable mind–body experience.

Whatever your interests or areas of study, studying ballet can enhance your life.

BALLET IN ACADEMIC SETTINGS

Dance courses have been longtime offerings in colleges, universities, and schools. Ballet classes are offered in dance, physical education, theater, music, or other departments. General education courses in a university, an introductory course in a major, a course in a public school curriculum, or a continuing education course include ballet and other dance forms. Beginning ballet is a foundational course for becoming a dancer or choreographer. Taking beginning ballet may lead you to continue your study of ballet, explore other dance forms, or continue to attend dance performances.

Students in academic ballet courses learn ballet technique, apply movement principles to class work, view ballet performances, and study ballet as a performing art. Similar to the methods of studying other art forms, students learn the vocabulary and technical terms of ballet, study its history, gain a sense of the dance form's aesthetics, and gain other supporting knowledge such as injury prevention and the requirements and expectations of a dancer. Testing entails both performance and written assignments.

Participating in ballet class challenges your body and your mind.

BALLET IN COMMUNITY SETTINGS

When individuals participate in an aesthetic type of physical activity such as ballet, they benefit from dancing and mental and social engagement. Although many dance opportunities focus on children, if you wish to extend your ballet studies into adulthood, you can try options such as the following:

- Dance studios
- Community parks and recreation programs
- Fitness centers
- Dance companies with schools
- Arts organizations

DID YOU KNOW?

In the United States, universities have offered beginning ballet courses since the early 1920s. The University of Nebraska at Lincoln was one of the first universities to offer a ballet course in the physical education department.

Explore your community and see what it has to offer in classes or performances. You can contribute to ballet as an art form by attending performances, volunteering or supporting community performances, and being an advocate for the arts in schools and your community.

BASICS OF BALLET CLASS

The main objective of a beginning ballet class is learning to dance. Thus, the class requires no previous experience and is structured differently from other academic subjects such as literature, chemistry, or social studies. The teacher presents the day's exercises and combinations, and then you as a student respond by replicating the movement to music. Attending class provides physical practice and intellectual knowledge on which you build your technique and understanding of ballet as an art form.

If you have had previous ballet training, you may be required to attend a placement class where instructors determine your level, or you may talk with your teacher about your previous training. Keep in mind that beginning ballet focuses on the foundations of ballet and steps you may have already learned. However, if you want to review the foundations to renew your body's movement memory or if you simply enjoy practicing the basics, then beginning ballet may be the right choice for you. No matter your level, attending class regularly helps you perfect your technique and develop your artistry.

Dance Studio

The dance studio is the space where dancers learn, practice, and refine technique. Generally it should be large enough to accommodate around 20 to 30 people moving comfortably. Most dance studios have high ceilings and hardwood or special vinyl dance floors. Full-length mirrors line one or more of the walls, and barres are attached along several walls. One corner may have a piano or sound system for accompaniment.

Teacher's Role

In the ballet class, the teacher is your guide to attaining technical competency. The teacher helps you learn ballet in the following ways:

- Building your beginning ballet vocabulary and technique
- Linking movement principles to ballet exercises, steps, positions, and poses
- Facilitating physical and intellectual connections to ballet as an art form
- Teaching you about ballet history, artists, styles, and aesthetics
- Providing opportunities for viewing and understanding ballet performance

Throughout the ballet class, the teacher presents exercises or combinations and students perform them. The teacher observes everyone's movement and provides feedback to the whole class or specific students to hone technique, to apply to performance, and for safety and clarity. The teacher may use a variety of teaching strategies to meet students' individual needs and learning goals. The teacher directs the students in a progression of steps while coordinating them with the music or musician.

Music and the Musician for Dance

The ballet teacher may either use prerecorded music or a musician for dance, usually a pianist, to accompany the dancers. The musician for dance coordinates with and complements the teacher to ensure that the ballet class runs smoothly and is an enjoyable learning experience. The musician for dance usually has a memorized repertoire of classical music from which to draw. This repertoire includes a variety of time signatures and tempos to match different parts of the class. Often classical music repertoire is augmented with popular, contemporary, and improvised works to provide diversity, change in mood or tempo, and enjoyment during the dance class.

The teacher guides the musician for dance to provide accompaniment that is appropriate for the dancers' level of study. The teacher directs the musician for dance throughout the class. For each exercise or combination, the teacher indicates the time signature, sets the tempo, and presents the movement either verbally or by demonstrating it to the class.

> **DID YOU KNOW?**
>
> Dance and music are sister arts. The music in the ballet class supports learning about movement and music while it enhances the classroom experience with the synergy between movement and music.

EXPECTATIONS AND ETIQUETTE FOR STUDENTS

Ballet class etiquette has evolved over centuries from its origins in royal courts and theater. (For more information on this evolution, see chapter 8, History of Ballet.)

Today's expectations for ballet etiquette are based on tradition; following them connects you to past generations of dancers. Protocols and rules allow the class to move efficiently through many exercises in the class. As in any class, these requirements support effective and efficient learning. Expectations for students in ballet class in an academic setting combine tradition, contemporary teaching strategies, and academic class requirements.

In class, you are expected to stand quietly while observing the teacher's demonstration of the exercises and combinations, then perform the movements as prompted by the teacher or later attend to the movement you are performing. Do not talk with other students during or between combinations. If you have a question, raise your hand after the teacher's explanation and before executing the combination. During class, dancers neither eat nor chew gum, and all dancers should show mutual respect for each other's personal space and performance times within the framework of ballet protocols and rules.

Be mindful in class so that you can develop your concentration to learn movements while they are presented. Listen to the teacher's explanation of the movements and counts. Attend to executing each part of the movement sequence to help you memorize it for

> ## DID YOU KNOW?
>
> In traditional ballet classes, men and women mirrored roles based on historical etiquette in society. For the center part of class, ladies stood in the front and gentlemen stood in the back. When moving across the floor, first the ladies would execute the combination, then the gentlemen would have their turn. Often, the music would change to a slower tempo to accommodate men's elevation in combinations in the center or for higher jumps and leaps across the floor. In a beginning ballet class, the teacher determines whether or not the class will follow tradition.

Students watch and listen as the teacher explains and demonstrates.

later recall and practice. Review the steps in your mind after class and before the next class meeting to further aid in learning. These strategies help you make adjustments and incorporate corrections to movement sequences as you learn them.

Consistently Attending Class

Attending every class is important because in each class period you learn new movements and information. Attendance at each class increases your movement vocabulary and knowledge, builds on previous material practiced, and highlights different combinations. Because you may learn several new exercises, steps, or poses during one class period, all the key points can be difficult to remember by the end of class and even more so by the next class, so attending every class ensures that you review or reinforce what you learned in previous classes. In a beginning ballet class, exercises and steps are not always presented in the same order as they appear in a standard ballet class. This sequence is adjusted as the class gains a working vocabulary of exercises and steps for each part of the course. Consistent attendance helps you keep up with these adjustments and not slow down the class trying to catch up.

Preparing and Practicing

When preparing for the next class, read this book and access the web resource that supplements each chapter to support and extend what you learned in the previous class. Yes, you get homework in ballet class, including both physical and mental practice and academic assignments.

You are responsible for learning and remembering the exercises and steps presented in previous classes. This enables the teacher to add more information to the content or for the class to move on to new material and therefore complete the course work for the beginning ballet class. Outside of class, practice the exercises and steps you learned. When you perform physical practice, the correct movement and the information about how to perform it become ingrained in your body and your mind, speeding up the learning process. Use the web resource as your personal tutor. It contains video clips and photos of exercises, steps, positions, and poses to help you learn and retain the immense amount of foundational material presented in a beginning ballet class.

Arriving on Time

The parts of the class are presented in a sequence, so it is important to be physically and mentally prepared to dance before the class begins. That means you should be dressed and ready to go when class begins. Being on time shows respect for the teacher and your classmates and it gives you time to get ready to fully participate in the class. To mentally prepare for ballet class, leave your previous class information and your personal cares at the door of the studio. You have come to dance and enjoy the experience. When you attend class, you commit to dance for the entire class period until the teacher dismisses the class.

If you are late to class, wait near the entrance of the studio until the teacher acknowledges you and asks you to join the class. If you arrive after a certain number of exercises at the barre have been executed, you may not be allowed to join the class. If you have to leave a class early, clear it with the teacher before the start of class. When it is time to leave, exit the studio quietly and unobtrusively between combinations so as not to disturb the flow of class. Your teacher will indicate specific requirements regarding entering the class late and exiting the class early.

If you have an emergency for which you need to leave during class, discretely talk with your teacher. Being tardy to class or leaving early for your next class should not be a recurring event. If you have to run to ballet class from across campus or to another class immediately after ballet, you need to determine a way to arrive before the ballet class begins or leave immediately after class. If you are having trouble because of scheduling conflicts, then discuss the situation with your instructors.

STRUCTURE OF BALLET CLASS

Today's ballet class structure evolved through history absorbing traditions, movement practices, and dance science. In a beginning ballet class, dancers learn basic exercises and steps and they perform simple combinations at slow tempos. They gain technique competency, learn movement principles, develop a professional attitude, and become aware of customary practices in a dance studio.

The ballet class is different from a lecture course or another arts class. The ballet class has two distinct parts: the barre and the center. During both parts of the class, dancers follow protocols and rules of etiquette to expedite transitions from one combination to another so that more class time can be spent dancing.

Barre

The **barre** has two meanings: It is a piece of equipment and it is a portion of the ballet class. A *barre* is a wooden or metal rail that is either attached to several walls of the studio or is a free-standing, portable structure placed across the studio space. *Barre* also refers to the series of exercises done at the barre to warm up and strengthen the body as preparation for the second part of class. In today's ballet class dancers often execute a series of pre-barre exercises that warm up the body and prepare them for performing the traditional barre exercises.

Whether you are a novice, experienced, or professional ballet dancer, executing barre is an essential part of ballet class. It prepares you for dancing during the second part of class. It establishes correct placement and it develops core and leg strength, directionality, balance, foot articulation, and weight transfer skills. Barre exercises help you to reconnect with the mind–body aspects of ballet and to deepen and refine your technique. The sequence of the barre exercises may differ depending on your teacher's training or association with a particular school or method of instruction.

Center

Once you have completed the barre exercises, you move to a place in the middle of the studio for the center portion of class. In the **center,** you learn steps, positions, and poses to gain a basic movement vocabulary of ballet. You repeat exercises from the barre and learn steps that develop into dynamic movement combinations without an outside means of support. In other words, in the center you apply what you learned at the barre and you learn to dance.

Center combinations vary in tempo and include various steps and poses in changing sequences to challenge you.

Parts of the center include the following:

- Center practice of selected exercises from the barre to refine technique, balance, and directionality
- Slow, or *adagio*, combinations include classical ballet poses, arm and foot positions, steps, and turns
- Fast, or *allegro*, combinations include small or large jumps, hops, and leaps that are performed either as short combinations moving side to side, front or back, or across the floor

In the beginning ballet class, exercises, steps, and sections of the class are not always introduced in the same order as they appear in a standard ballet class. By the end of the term, the standard barre and center will have emerged.

The teacher may designate groups of three or four dancers to perform combinations in the center so that everyone has space to dance. The first group takes their places in the middle of the studio to begin. The second and additional groups stand and wait their turn at the side or back of the studio. After the first group completes the combination, the musician for dance may perform a vamp or repetition of the music to cue the first group to exit to one side and the second group to take its place. This rotation of groups continues until everyone has executed the combination.

The teacher may have dancers perform combinations across the floor in lines, groups, duets, or solo from side to side in the studio or on the diagonal beginning at a back corner and traveling to the opposite front corner. Dancers in the first group should get about a third to halfway across the floor, which is usually 8 or more measures of music before the second group begins. The time between groups helps to alleviate any collisions and still keep the class moving across the floor.

When crossing the floor in lines parallel to the front of the classroom, it is easy to go to the end of the line so that the combination can start again. When performing the combination on the other side and moving across the floor in the opposite direction in a line or on a diagonal, often the second row of dancers or second group must move forward to lead the combination.

When waiting your turn to execute a combination in the center or across the floor, stand quietly and observe your peers. Most often dancers stand at the side of the studio toward the back. If the teacher permits, you may mark, or physically move through the combination, or mentally review the combinations. Practicing the combination mentally is an effective way to learn movement. While waiting your turn, try visualizing the steps, directions, and other elements of the combination in time to the music.

Révérence

At the end of the traditional ballet class, dancers perform a **révérence,** a short combination in the center in which men bow and women curtsy, to thank the teacher and the musician for dance, if your class has one, and say good-bye. The ballet class ends with students applauding the teacher and musician for dance.

Cool-Down

Cool-down exercises include slow movements and stretches that allow your body and mind to relax and regain balance before leaving the studio. Slowly stretching your muscles increases flexibility and helps your body recover from the work in class. Teachers determine when or whether to include a cool-down in class. Sometimes they have you perform stretching exercises between the barre and center, either at the barre or on the floor. They may have you cool down after the center either before or after class is officially over, when the body is warm from performing combinations across the floor. If your teacher does not include a cool-down, you may choose to do personal stretching after class before you leave the studio.

LEARNING AND PERFORMING BALLET

Ballet is a physical activity; therefore, ballet performance requires muscular strength, flexibility, and coordination. Ballet is also an intense mental and intellectual pursuit that requires concentration, focus, and attention to detail. Developing the ability to read the body in stillness, through movements, and in relation to others who are moving through the same space takes years of practice. While moving, dancers must quickly apply concepts such as technique, etiquette, movement principles, protocols, rules, and style while weaving in their own artistry and personality to create art. The mental side of ballet is equally challenging to the physical aspects of the art. When you encounter challenges in performing ballet, don't give up. Remember that all aspects of ballet are naturally challenging and your dedication to study and practice will lead you to make progress.

SUMMARY

In the studio dancers learn to move fluidly through space and slowly through time. They learn to seemingly control or defy gravity while moving at great speed or contrast it with a slow elegance of continuous lines and shapes drawn in space. Dancers return to the studio on a regular basis to hone and perfect their technique, trying to attain flawless performance and sophisticated interconnection of dance with the music as they continue in their quest for perfection.

Learning ballet requires commitment, perseverance, and personal dedication to developing excellence in yourself and your performance. Participating in a ballet class is a ritual for the dancer—novice to professional—grounded in history and tradition.

To find supplementary materials for this chapter such as learning activities, e-journaling assignments, and web links, visit the web resource at www.HumanKinetics.com/BeginningBallet1E.

Chapter *2*

Preparing for Class

Preparing for ballet class can have several meanings. Ballet class dress requirements vary, as do classes. By putting on your dancewear, you create an outward transformation that helps you get into the frame of mind for dance class—your attire, shoes, gear, and physical appearance make you look and feel like a ballet dancer. Being aware of ballet class structure, traditions, and etiquette also prepares you for participating in the dance milieu. Additionally, awareness of the connection between your body and mind prepares your senses for dance. You think like a dancer when you prepare yourself both mentally and physically. This chapter covers what you need to do and think about before entering class. Some content in this chapter comes from ballet tradition; other content refers to contemporary practices.

DRESSING FOR CLASS

Ballet classes have specific clothing and grooming requirements for men and women. Your teacher usually indicates these requirements at your first class. Dancers wear practice clothing that has evolved over centuries and ranges from traditional to the latest styles. Dancewear is form fitting and may be a different style than your personal style of clothing or your comfort level. Practice clothing is required for class for several reasons, including the following:

- It allows you to move easily as you execute ballet exercises and steps through your full range of motion.
- It reveals your posture and body lines in poses and when moving through space.
- It allows you and the teacher to check and correct technical and aesthetic elements if necessary.

If this is your first time purchasing dancewear, try to shop for your clothes at your local dance shop rather than order them online. Ballet practice clothes come in a range of fabrics, colors, and styles. Some may be more appealing to you than others. When purchasing dancewear, think about the number of classes you will be taking each week. Practice clothing should be washed after class, so if you can afford it, buy one outfit for each weekly class so that you have to wash your dancewear only once a week.

Practice Attire for Women

The dress code for your class will help determine choices of practice clothing. The classic ballet practice outfit for women is a black leotard and pink or beige tights. Modern versions are a black leotard and black tights or a unitard, which provides a flattering continuous line to the body.

When selecting a leotard, you have some fashion choices. Decide if you would be most comfortable in a tank-style, short-sleeved, or long-sleeved leotard. Choose either a scoop or V neckline style to flatter your body type. Take into consideration that you will be moving throughout the class and your body will get warm. Also, the studio may be air-conditioned or the windows may be opened. Leotard leg openings are usually cut high to make the legs appear longer. Regardless of the style of leg opening you select, opt for maximum coverage across the hips.

Professional dance tights are designed to withstand the rigors of ballet. They are made of nylon, spandex, or similar fabric with adequate stretch, elastic waistband, and resistance to sagging. Ballet tights may have seams down the back or they may be seamless. They can be footed or convertible (with an opening on the sole of the foot). Put on your tights as you would fine hosiery: Gather the tight leg to near the toe and pull it on. Stretch the tight up each leg so that it fits snugly.

Fashion tights may be a tempting option because of variety and price, but you should invest in tights designed specifically for dance. Fashion tights are for fashion, not for dance class. They are not made to stretch in the ways that dancers move or to withstand multiple washings, they are often thin, and they may bag at the ankles.

You also have choices for what to wear under your leotard. A bra is a must for support because of the physical activity involved. The choice and style should provide good support, full coverage, and comfort under the leotard. Many leotards have built-in bras. If support and cut are critical, wear the bra you plan to wear for dance class when shopping for a leotard. Female dancers wear tights without underwear. If you feel more comfortable wearing panties under your tights, first check your course dress code to determine whether panties are allowed and then select a neutral color and a comfortable style that does not show from under your high-cut leotard.

For ballet class, women usually wear pink or beige ballet slippers similar to the color of their tights. If you wear black tights, then wear black shoes. Check with your teacher to determine your options. For more information, see Selecting and Fitting Ballet Slippers later in this chapter.

> **DID YOU KNOW?**
>
> In the Dance Theatre of Harlem, dancers wear flesh-colored tights for classical ballets. Each dancer wears tights that closely match the dancer's skin tone.

Hairstyles

For the classic ballet hairstyle, all hair, including bangs and wisps, should be pulled off your face and secured into a bun in the back of the head. Flying hair could interfere with your movement and hit you or others in the face. If you have thick or very long hair, try braiding your ponytail before securing it with several clips or barrettes to the back of the head. Putting a net over your bun or braid keeps it smooth before securing it. For short hair, clip bangs away from your face and wear a headband. For medium-length hair, you can choose to put it in a ponytail, cover it with a net, pin it, clip it in a bun, or put it in a French roll and secure it with pins.

To hold your hair in place, check that pins are secure. Crisscrossing pins helps to keep them secure. Losing pins and stepping on them in class are neither comfortable nor safe situations for dancers in class. If you typically lose pins in class, opt for larger pins or a clip. Hair spray ensures your hair and any wisps are pulled into your smooth hairstyle.

Jewelry

Wearing jewelry in ballet class is not encouraged, mainly for safety reasons. If you wear jewelry, it could hit you or another person while you are moving. During turns or jumps, a necklace, bracelet, or watch could hit you or another dancer or get caught in clothing. Large and dangly earrings can get caught in clothing or hair and can be a safety concern. Small pierced earrings such as studs or small hoops are safer and therefore usually acceptable. To avoid loss or damage, leave your jewelry at home before you go to class rather than put it in a locker or dance bag after you get there.

Practice Outfit for Men

The classic ballet practice outfit for men is a pair of black tights with a black leotard or black or white T-shirt. Your instructor may allow different colors and styles. T-shirts with logos, messages, and images may not be considered appropriate dress for ballet class. The leotard should snugly fit the body and stretch to meet the demands of dance movement. The T-shirt should fit the body closely and be long enough to easily tuck into the tights. Leotards offer a smoother body line, while T-shirts may become baggy. Another option is a unitard, which can help you achieve a long, smooth body line. If you are uncomfortable with wearing the traditional ballet attire, check with your instructor about clothing alternatives. Some instructors allow male students to wear bike pants or tight jazz pants to ballet class. The dress code for your class will dictate your choices of practice clothing.

Men's tights are cut to fit men's bodies. They are made of the same fabrics as women's but of a thicker weight or a heavier denier. The classic style is to wear footed tights, but footless tights are also an option. Tights should be able to stretch several inches above the waist so that you can wear a belt or heavy, wide elastic and then fold the tights over the belt several times for a smooth look. A webbed belt made of strong fabric with a smooth buckle can be adjusted to your waist size yet not snag the tight fabric.

A dance belt is the undergarment for the male dancer. Similar to an athletic support, the dance belt is specifically designed for dance and worn underneath the tights. The dance belt is critical for support and a necessary part of the male dancer's attire in class and on stage. When you dress for class, put on the dance belt first, the leotard next, and the tights last.

These students are properly dressed for ballet class.

Traditionally men wear white socks over the tights. If you wear a black unitard you can wear either white or black socks, depending on the color of your ballet shoes or teacher's preference. If you wear footless tights or footless unitard, you can wear socks or go barefoot in your shoes. Wearing shoes without socks may not be as comfortable because the socks absorb perspiration.

Men's ballet shoes can be either black or white. If you wear a large shoe size, you might have to special order your shoes through a dance shop. In this case it is important to have a trained salesperson fit you for the correct size and width because special-order shoes often cannot be returned. For more information, see Selecting and Fitting Ballet Slippers later in this chapter.

> **DID YOU KNOW?**
>
> When you go to purchase your first pair of ballet shoes, wear a pair of the tights or, for men, the socks you plan to wear in class to ensure a proper fit.

Whether you have long or short hair, keep it away from your face. If your hair is long, you may wear a bandanna or headband to keep hair out of your eyes. If your hair is long enough to tie back, secure it in a ponytail.

FOOT CARE

Ballet class gives the feet an intense workout, so dancers' feet require specific care. Always keep your feet clean and smooth. If your feet have corns, calluses, or rough spots, use a foot soak and regularly massage foot cream on your feet to help soften the skin. Keep your toenails clipped to an appropriate length—long enough to avoid ingrown toenails and short enough to avoid discomfort and snagging on your tights and shoes. Cut toenails straight across.

CARRYING DANCE GEAR

Use a dance bag to carry your clothes, shoes, and other items to and from class. Bags can become heavy when they contain a collection of stuff you rarely need or use, so make wise choices about what you need for before and after class. Items to consider include the following:

- Towel
- Deodorant
- Adhesive bandages
- Manicure scissors or toenail clippers
- Safety pins
- Hair clips, pins, ponytail holders, hairnets, and headbands
- A separate bag for wet or used practice clothing

◆ Personal grooming items and an extra towel if you plan to shower after class

After class, it is easy to dump your wet dance clothes and shoes into your dance bag, zip it, and go. If your ballet class is early in the day or the weather is warm, separate your damp practice clothes from your shoes and other items in your dance bag. Remove the damp items, air out your shoes, and leave your dance bag open before packing for your next dance class.

SELECTING AND FITTING BALLET SLIPPERS

Ballet shoes, or slippers, are essential to your ability to learn and perform in class. They are the most important equipment you will need. Choosing the right shoe is important, as is getting the proper fit. Your instructor will provide suggestions and preferences for ballet shoes. If possible, go to your local dancewear shop to get a trained person to fit you. Buying a pair of ballet shoes from a regular shoe store is not the same as getting properly fitted for ballet slippers in a dance shop. Ballet shoes are critical for your performance and safety.

Ballet shoes must fit properly. This is critical for your safety and performance quality. Ballet slippers have been used for centuries with only a few innovations in construction to increase comfort and flexibility. Your ballet slippers ensure safe movement throughout class. Well-fitting slippers play a part in developing your arch, pointed foot, and flexibility in ballet footwork. They also play a part in how you look because the foot is a focal point of the dancer's body in ballet. Movement of the foot either initiates or ends the line of the leg that then radiates through the entire body when executing ballet poses and movements.

Ballet slippers are lightweight, soft, and made of either leather or canvas. Leather is more expensive than canvas, but it lasts longer. Slippers come in shades of pink, beige, white, or black. Do not wear your ballet slippers outside of class; they are designed exclusively for dancing in the dance studio.

Your ballet slippers must fit like a glove to your foot, so when you purchase your ballet slippers, try them on with the tights that you plan to wear in class. If you don't wear tights during class, try them on barefoot. Generally, ballet slippers are sized one to two and a half sizes smaller than street shoes. When you try on slippers, stand up and put your weight on both feet. Your toes should be straight and reach the end of the shoe. Each slipper should fit snugly along the sides and across the toes. If your toes turn under, then the slipper is too short. If it feels snug but your toes are straight, don't worry; it will relax and stretch slightly as you dance in it. If your toes do not lay flat in the shoe, try a wider size. During the fitting, point and flex your feet. If your heel starts to slip out of the slipper when you stand or walk a few steps, you may need to move up a size. Your heel should extend a bit off the back of the sole.

Ballet slippers do not have right- and left-foot designations, but as you wear them, they conform to your feet. Be sure to try them on both feet. It is not unusual for people to have one foot larger than the other, so check that both slippers fit before you purchase them.

If you have to return your ballet slippers for any reason, they should look just as they did when you got them out of the box for the first time. Until you or your instructor confirm that they fit, try your ballet slippers while wearing tights and stand on the paper that they are wrapped in or the inside top of the shoe box. The soles can pick up dirt from floors.

Parts of the Ballet Slipper

Knowing the parts of the slipper (figure 2.1) helps you understand what to consider when purchasing slippers and adjusting them for your foot. The slipper sole is made of either stiff leather or suede that stretches from the ball of the foot to under the heel. For beginners who are learning to use their feet, the single-sole style is the primary choice. The split-sole style is a more appropriate choice for a dancer with a developed foot, but it can be a matter of the instructor's preference.

Regardless of material, the slipper should conform to your foot without bulges or gaps. Around the opening of the slipper a casing encloses either a cloth drawstring or elastic cord. The casing opens at the front of the slipper, or vamp. The cord is the mechanism for tightening the slipper to fit your foot.

> **DID YOU KNOW?**
>
> The first ballet dancers danced in high-heeled shoes. During the 18th century, female dancers removed the heels from their shoes for dancing. Throughout much of the first part of the 20th century, female dancers used ribbons wrapped around their ankles instead of elastic.

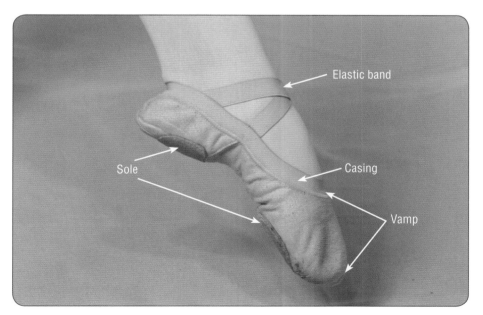

Figure 2.1 Parts of the ballet slipper. This example shows a split-sole slipper, but slippers can also be single soled.

Tightening the Slipper

To tighten your ballet slipper, slip it on and move to a kneeling position on one leg with the slipper flat on the floor. Alternatively, you can stand with one foot on a bench. To tighten the cord, cross the ends and then pull gently away from the slipper. The cord should not tighten so that it cuts into your forefoot or heel. Once you have determined the tightness, double-knot the cord. Take off the slipper, then slightly stretch the ends of the cord and tuck them inside the slipper. You may have to move them around a bit until they fit into the slipper. For safety reasons, tying the cord in a bow is not recommended. The bow can come untied and become a tripping hazard. For aesthetic reasons, a bow breaks the clean line of the foot and the shoe. After the first class or two, check whether you need to tighten your cords again. To ensure that you have room to loosen them later if needed, do not tighten the cords only once and then cut. If you cut the cords too short, they could retreat into the casing and you would need to purchase a new pair of slippers. Be conservative and keep the cords long until your shoes conform to your feet.

Using Elastic Bands

Some ballet slippers come with an elastic band already sewn at the center side seam. However, you should opt for slippers without elastics so that you can sew them on. This may sound like a lot of trouble, especially if you don't sew, but it's worth having a custom fit. The elastic on a ballet slipper should be sewn around the ankle on an angle. Ballet slippers often come with unattached elastic, or you can purchase it separately in the store. Most dancewear stores carry colored elastic made specifically for the ballet slippers they sell. Choose whether to use one or two bands across your foot, and consider this choice when determining the length of elastic you will need.

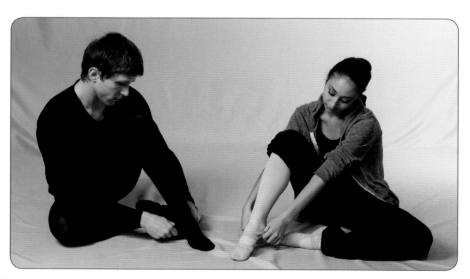

These students are putting on their ballet shoes for class.

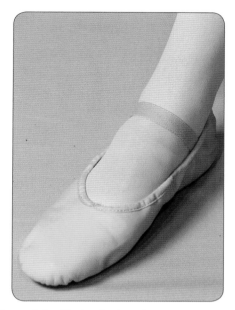

Figure 2.2 Single-elastic style.

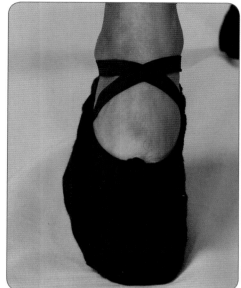

Figure 2.3 Crisscross style.

Sewing the elastic band begins with dividing the elastic either in half or into four equal lengths if you use the crisscross method. Each elastic length should be long enough to cross your instep near the ankle and extend about half an inch below the fabric casing or binding that contains the cord that tightens your shoes. You can sew the elastic in one of two ways: single or crisscross.

For a single elastic style, sew a single elastic band close to the ankle (see figure 2.2). To find the proper place to sew the elastic, take your slipper and fold in the entire back from where the heel begins down onto the inside sole. Then mark the spot where the fold touches. This is where you should place the elastic. Hold the elastic in place on this forward angle, then sew it securely around all sides using double thread. Be sure to sew only the fabric casing and the interior cloth of the shoe.

Using two elastic pieces that crisscross (figure 2.3) is popular with male dancers and with female dancers who have narrow feet. The elastic crosses the instep on a diagonal. Sew one end of it near the ankle as for the single-elastic style and sew the other end on the opposite side near the middle of the instep. Attach the second elastic in a similar manner on the other side of the slipper.

PREPARING YOURSELF MENTALLY AND PHYSICALLY

Dressing for class helps you attain the appearance of a dancer, but it is only part of preparing for class; you also need mental and physical preparation. To give yourself adequate time to prepare your mind and body for class, make a habit of arriving to the studio early.

Mental Preparation

Fully enjoying the ballet class experience requires getting in the right frame of mind to learn and retain the material presented during the class. This mental preparation begins before you enter the studio. Actually, the mental preparation for your ballet class begins as you walk to your class. This is a good time to put away the massive information you just learned in chemistry or economics class, or those everyday to-do lists, and empty your mind in preparation for class. You need to give yourself time to make the transition to prepare for ballet class. This is an important practice. An open mind puts you in a neutral place where you can concentrate on experiencing and remembering the movement or sequence of movements. This practice helps the beginning dancer to develop a visual and kinesthetic memory, which is essential for learning dance.

Some dancers believe that clearing your mind and giving your undivided focus is therapeutic mentally and physically. A clear mind takes your thoughts away from all the information clutter that can easily take over your thinking. Taking some deep breaths and coming to a neutral place will help you to be attentive and perhaps more relaxed when preparing for class. Being on time and mentally prepared for any class is critical for getting the most out of it. This is especially true of dance class.

Memorizing Movements During Class

Your study of ballet begins with a few short exercises and steps. As you progress, the number and variety expand into many complex combinations, so you must develop your movement memory. In the beginning your teacher moves with you so that you can follow along. In class, carefully observe movements and begin to recognize steps or patterns. When the teacher no longer moves with you through an exercise, step, or combination, you are expected to know and be able to execute the movements on your own. Resist the temptation to follow another dancer in the mirror or in front of you; instead, recall the sequence from memory. When you imitate another dancer's movement, you miss out on experiencing the movement in your own unique way and you rob yourself of the opportunity to develop your movement memory.

Recalling Movements for the Next Class

What you learn in one class often becomes the basis for what you learn in the next class, so you must be able to recall previous movement sequences. If you are unable to perform a sequence at the next class meeting, then class time is spent reviewing material and not moving forward.

To develop your ability to recall movements, first visualize the movement sequence. Then, physically practice the sequence while saying the action terms or ballet terms to yourself. Determine which movements are unclear and practice the missing parts. Use the videos and photos on the web resource to help refresh your memory about specific exercises or steps.

If you need help, ask another student in class about the exercise, step, or combination. If you have questions after class, do not hesitate to ask the teacher to explain the sequence. It is better to take the time to learn the movement correctly than to have to relearn it later. Remembering movement is the basis for developing a visual memory. It is linked to physical attributes such as seeing movement patterns and developing a movement memory.

Physical Preparation

Your body must be prepared for each part of the ballet class. Although the class sequence is designed to progress logically from one exercise to the next, every body is different and has its own unique needs for preparation. If you have had an injury in the past, get to class early to warm up the body parts that need special attention. You can do your personal warm-up either sitting on the floor or standing at the barre. Stretch your muscles only after the body is warmed up through the barre exercises or at the end of class. Do not walk into the studio and throw your leg onto the highest barre or do a split on the floor without a proper warm-up.

Often in academic classes, the class ends and you rush out to your next class. Academic ballet classes may or may not include a cool-down. If possible, make time to perform slow stretching movements on the floor or at the barre before you leave. This will help the body recover properly and therefore be better prepared for the next class.

Mind–Body Preparation

In ballet class you focus on physically executing movement sequences while applying proper technique and ballet principles. When you practice coordinating multiple elements in time to the music, you engage in an external and an internal self-checking process. Therefore, your mind and body need to work together as a unit.

Gaining Spatial Sense

As a beginning dancer, you should develop spatial sense to tell where your body and its parts are in space. Ballet directions are more complex than simply front, side, and back. Arm and leg directions have direct relationships to body parts, and the whole body has a relationship to the space surrounding it. Further, the relationships change as you move through space, so you need to develop an acute spatial sense. Spatial sense contributes to your awareness of body line.

Seeing Movement Patterns

When you keenly observe movements in class, you can recognize patterns in them. Then executing them mindfully helps you to memorize movement sequences. One exercise or step can include several parts. When you observe the teacher you should first see the body as a whole and then focus on the parts that are moving or nonmoving.

In beginning ballet, a movement sequence begins with the dancer in a specific position, an introductory arm movement, and then a series of leg movements. The legs are either straight or bent and move in different directions and at different heights. At the barre, the dancer is most often stationary with leg movements in different directions and heights. In the center, the leg movements propel you slow or fast in different paths through space or across the floor.

Developing Your Kinesthetic Sense

In dance, as in other arts, you use your five senses. However, the focus often moves quickly from one sense to another. **Kinesthetic sense** is defined as muscle, bone, and joint sense.

As a beginning dancer your visual understanding of the movements in an exercise or step is primary; it helps you replicate that movement with your body. Next, you apply your aural sense when you replicate the movement in relation to the timing and the music. Developing a feeling for your body's parts and their relationships to each other is key to a kinesthetic sense. As you gain experience in ballet, you develop this sense. To advance as a dancer, you must learn to transfer your visual perception of correct position or movement to an internal feeling with which you just know what is correct. These levels of learning take time, so have some patience with yourself and your movement learning curve.

SUMMARY

Preparing for ballet class helps you in many ways. Knowing your teacher's expectations is a must. Using appropriate clothing and equipment helps you look and feel like a ballet dancer. Selecting well-fitted ballet slippers enhances your performance and comfort. Preparing mentally and physically helps you learn, retain, and improve your dance skills. Take the time and energy to prepare; it's worth the effort.

To find supplementary materials for this chapter such as learning activities, e-journaling assignments, and web links, visit the web resource at www.HumanKinetics.com/BeginningBallet1E.

3

Safety and Health

Ballet is a demanding physical activity that requires attention to safety and health. The safety and health considerations covered in this chapter apply to ballet and other dance forms; they are all factors related to a physically active lifestyle.

Studio safety begins with wearing proper attire and footwear, practicing correct technique, and applying ballet protocols in class. Personal safety includes proper grooming, awareness of personal space, and understanding how healthy lifestyle choices support your dance experience. Practicing correct technique requires a basic understanding of dance anatomy and kinesiology, body types, and injury prevention. As your ballet course progresses, classes become faster paced with more information to absorb.

To be safe, you need to be aware of how you move and where you move in the space. This mindset helps you even more as you take on more responsibility for your work in class. For optimal performance in class and quick postclass recovery, you need to practice proper nutrition and hydration.

Although your teacher can help you to practice safely throughout class, keeping your body safe is ultimately your responsibility.

STUDIO SAFETY

Dance studios are located in various places, such as dance schools, high schools, and university campuses, and they are configured in various ways. For example, sometimes locker areas adjoin the studio space and sometimes they are a distance away. A variety of elements contribute to general safety in the studio.

Dance studios are busy places with large groups of people coming and going between classes. For your personal safety and to protect your belongings, you should always be aware of your surroundings. Know the evacuation routes from the studio, locker room, and building and know where you should go in case of weather emergencies such as earthquakes or tornado warnings.

Equipment and Storage

Before class, be sure the dance space is clear of any items that are not essential for your class. If you move portable barres during class, store them together at one side of the studio so as not to interfere with group entrances and exits for combinations in the middle of the studio or pathways across the floor. If you are allowed to bring your dance bag into the studio, store it out of the way of entrances, exits, and class activities.

Climate Control

The climate in the studio affects your health and your ballet experience. When a large group of people move in a studio space, the temperature rises. Ventilation, air conditioning, and fans can help keep the studio air from getting too stifling or stagnant and help keep you from getting overheated.

Floors

Dance studio floors come in a wide range of materials, including wood and vinyl flooring developed specifically for dance. Studio floors should be clean and free of residue from cleaning agents so that they are not sticky or slippery. Slipping is a concern as you move across the floor or change directions in combinations. Related to floors is the condition of your shoe soles. Avoid wearing street shoes in the studio, and wear your ballet slippers only in the studio and related spaces. Before you enter the studio, check that the soles of your slippers are clean and dry to prevent slipping when moving and provide traction when landing.

PERSONAL SAFETY

When you take a ballet class, you participate in vigorous physical activity with many other students whose bodies are moving through space, sometimes very quickly; therefore, you should ensure your personal safety as well as the safety of others in the studio.

Personal safety begins with dressing and grooming for the ballet class. It includes dressing in proper clothing and wearing well-fitting shoes (see chapter 2). Clothing should fit close to the body and shoes should properly fit for both length and width. Too

SAFETY TIP ▶▶▶▶▶▶▶▶▶

To clean your ballet slippers, wipe the soles with a clean, damp cloth. Then let them air dry before you put them in your dance bag.

much length at the toes invites tripping over the end of your ballet slippers. When tightening your slippers, always tuck elastic cords into the slipper; tying them into a bow is potentially unsafe because they can come loose. As discussed in chapter 2, wearing little or no jewelry is a good choice for class. As you move, jewelry could cause injury to you or to others. Women with long hair should secure it in a bun or with a clip. A long ponytail or braid can hit you or other students as you move.

Personal Space

Understanding your **personal space** needs during different sections of the class is critical to your safety and enjoyment as well as that of your classmates. Your personal space accommodates leg, arm, and body extensions without entering your neighbors' space as you stand in one place and as you move through the studio space. The general space in the studio is a shared space with other dancers as they move as individuals or in groups at the barre, in the center, and across the floor.

Dancers spread out across the studio in their personal space to perform the center part of the class.

ACTIVITY

Determining Your Personal Space

Stand in a place that has no barriers to movement. Extend your arms overhead, then out to the sides of your body. Extend each leg forward, then to the side and to the back. Finally, turn around yourself. You have outlined a somewhat spherical space. This is the amount of space you will need to execute movements in place. Think about yourself moving within your sphere in relation to other students moving in side-to-side and forward-and-back patterns in the middle of the studio or moving in groups of two or three across the floor either in a line or on a diagonal.

If you don't regard your personal space and that of others in the class, you increase the likelihood of hitting someone near you. Think about 30 people in one class vigorously moving close to each other: Arms and legs moving and bodies turning can quickly lead to a collision. This situation intensifies if you wear jewelry. Even when in smaller groups or moving across the floor, you must be aware of your personal space and its relation to others at all times to avoid unintended physical contact and potential injury.

Personal Health Information

Personal health information is just that—personal information. If you have had an injury, surgery, or chronic health condition that might affect your physical performance or the health of your classmates, you are not obligated to tell everyone, but you should tell your instructor. To protect privacy, usually teachers encourage students to see them after the first class. Your teacher should be aware of any chronic condition or disease such as asthma, diabetes, or epilepsy in order to be prepared for a possible emergency.

Continued practice of safety rules helps you stay safe and build confidence. As you become more aware of sharing and moving in the space with other dancers, you may identify and be able to avoid dangerous situations in the class. In turn, this safety mindset contributes to your development of a professional attitude as a dancer.

BASIC ANATOMY AND KINESIOLOGY

Understanding basic anatomy of the bones, joints, and muscles and how they work underlies health and safety for dance. As a dancer, your body is your instrument and movement is your medium. Knowing anatomy and kinesiology helps you gain a deeper understanding of ballet technique from the inside out and the outside in. This synergy of body knowledge and technical knowledge supports healthy, strong, and safe dancing.

Anatomy

Anatomy is the study of the structure and function of the body, including its bones, muscles, and joints. Bones provide support for the body and act as levers. Muscles connect to other muscles with ligaments. Skeletal muscles move the bones and ligaments stabilize the joints where movement occurs.

Bones

The adult human body has 206 bones in various shapes and sizes. They play a part in movement, protect vital organs, produce blood cells, and store nutrients. The bones of the skeleton, their alignment, and the positioning of the spine, arms, and legs are integral to understanding how movement emanates through the muscles and joints. Alignment in ballet is a foundational movement principle that is dependent on skeletal alignment and positioning of the spine, head, arms, and legs to achieve a classical posture.

Skeletal Muscles

Skeletal muscles move the skeleton. They contract, or shorten, to move bones at the joints. They attach to bones by tendons. Skeletal muscles come in four types:

1. *Agonists* contract to produce movement.
2. *Antagonists* relax or lengthen while the agonists move.
3. *Synergists* either help control the movement or neutralize it.
4. *Stabilizers* hold certain muscles to support other movements.

All types of skeletal muscle function to create shape, stability, and movement in the dancer's body.

Joints

A joint is the location at which two or more bones meet. Bones attach to bones by ligaments. The body has three main types of joints:

1. *Ball and socket joints,* such as the hip or the shoulder
2. *Hinge joints,* such as the knee
3. *Gliding joints,* such as between the vertebrae and ribs, which have little capacity for movement
4. *Saddle joints,* such as at the base of the thumb
5. *Pivot joints,* such as between the upper portion of the forearm bones
6. *Condyloid joints,* such as in the wrist

Joint actions include a variety of movements, such as the following:

- *Flexion* (bending) and *extension* (straightening)
- *Abduction* (moving away from the center line of the body) and *adduction* (moving toward the center line of the body)

Table 3.1 Joint Actions

Action	Movement	Example
Flexion	Bending, folding of a joint	Hip flexion: Front of hip bending with grand battement devant
Extension	Straightening of a joint	Elbow straightening when in a push-up position
Abduction	Moving away from the center line of the body	Arms à la seconde: Arms moving from alongside the body to second position
Adduction	Moving toward the center line of the body	Assemblé: Legs coming together
External rotation	Rotating outward	Turning out from the hips for a grand plié in second position
Internal rotation	Rotating inward	Shoulder joint internally rotating to place the hand on the hip
Plantar flexion	Pointing the foot	Extending the leg and pointing the foot in battement tendu or dégagé
Dorsiflexion	Flexing the foot	Rocking back on the heels, lifting the forefoot

Adapted, by permission, from J.G. Haas, 2010, *Dance anatomy* (Champaign, IL: Human Kinetics), 3.

- *External rotation* (rotating outward) and *internal rotation* (rotating inward)
- *Plantar flexion* (pointing the foot) and *dorsiflexion* (flexing the foot)

Table 3.1 provides a summary of joint actions and examples of the movements associated with them.

Turnout

Turnout is a hallmark of ballet technique. In the beginning ballet class, dancers start with natural turnout, which creates an angle of approximately 90 degrees; each foot is turned out about 45 degrees. The external, or outward, rotation of the legs and feet begins at the hip socket. The kneecap should line up directly over the foot and the knee should fall over the second and third toes. The ankle should be perpendicular to the floor so that the foot does not roll inward or outward.

As the legs and feet gain strength and improved control, turnout can increase naturally. However, this change takes time. To keep the body safe, the degree of turnout should not be forced beyond natural turnout. When turnout is forced beyond the external rotation of the dancer's hips, several types of injuries can occur depending on where the force is applied. If the feet accept a position that is beyond the rotation of the hip socket, then the feet pronate (roll in) and cause the knees to move forward of the feet. This in turn can cause the pelvis to tilt backward instead of be perpendicular to the floor or to be tucked under and forward beyond proper alignment. Thus, forcing turnout over time can cause problems in the feet, knees, and pelvis. Strive to perform correct turnout to contribute to safe and injury-free dancing.

Physical Attributes

During the first days of class, the teacher observes each student to ascertain body types, knee variances, and foot differences. Knowing your physical attributes can help you determine how to move safely while practicing good technique.

All dancers—even professionals—come in various shapes and sizes. Dancers' bodies can be tall and slender, short and compact, or anything in between. Each body type has positive factors and inherent constraints.

Body Types

Dancers with an ectomorph body type have long limbs and slender figures, are flexible, and can move easily. To balance their natural capabilities, they should engage in activities to attain strength and endurance.

Dancers with a mesomorph body type have an athletic build that is muscular and compact and they have high levels of strength and endurance. These dancers excel in strong jumps and powerful movements through the air but must constantly work to increase flexibility.

Dancers with an endomorph body type have a round shape, move quickly, and possess strength and flexibility. These dancers must work hard to control body weight and increase endurance.

Although these descriptions present the general characteristics of each body type, people typically have a combination of body types. Body proportions of torso and leg length must also be considered. In classical ballet a body with a short torso and long legs allows for easier leg extensions and more flexibility, whereas a body with a long torso and short legs makes leg extensions more difficult. Nevertheless, regardless of body type, everyone can enjoy the benefits of ballet.

Knee Differences

Knee joints usually allow for one of two shapes in the legs: curved inward (bow-legged) or curved outward (knock-kneed). Dancers who have **bowlegs** have a space between the knees when standing with the insides of the feet together. Bowlegs are more prevalent in men than in women. Dancers with this knee type are strong and excel at jumping but most often have less flexibility. These dancers' feet often roll outward (supinate) with the body weight. The dancer should adjust for this misalignment to lessen the risk of injury on the inside of the knee.

Knock-knees are instantly recognized when standing with heels touching and legs outwardly rotated. The knees touch and calves either touch or nearly touch. For dancers with this knee type, the body weight gravitates to the heels. The knock-kneed dancer is flexible and typically has feet with a high arch; however, she must work at acquiring speed and elevation in jumps.

With both knee types, **hyperextension** occurs because as the knees press backward, ligaments behind the knees permanently stretch. As a result, dancers carry the weight of the body on the heels, which directly affects acquiring speed and elevation in jumps. The amount of hyperextension can be considered either a positive or negative attribute. Overall hyperextension plays a larger role in the body's alignment because it causes a rippling effect of adjustments that automatically occur to keep the body vertical. Characteristics of hyperextension include the following:

+ The head is forward.
+ The shoulders are back.
+ The ribs are released forward.
+ The hips are back and the lower back is arched (swayback).

Realigning the body and its parts with awareness of knee variances helps the body move more efficiently.

Foot Differences

Feet come in all shapes and sizes, such as long and narrow or short and compact. Types of arches include a high arch with a prominent forefoot, a compact arch, and a low arch or flatfoot. The arch of the foot contributes to the foot's flexibility and articulation as it moves from a full-foot position to full point on the floor or in the air.

The feet are a major focus in ballet because they create the foundation of support for the body through their positions. The feet execute ballet exercises and steps. Using your feet correctly is paramount to proper technique and injury prevention. How the foot is used contributes to the aesthetic quality of dance because it continues the line of the leg.

PREVENTING AND TREATING COMMON DANCE INJURIES

As with any sport or other physical activity, dance has specific injuries. Using your body to do vigorous and precise movements that you may not have done before can leave you vulnerable to injury. The most common dance injuries in a ballet class are blisters, strains, and sprains.

Blisters

A blister is a result of shoes that may be too tight or rub the heel or a toe. Blisters can become infected, so take steps to prevent and treat them. Before you enter the studio, ensure that your ballet slippers have a snug yet comfortable fit. Check that the seams on your tights and drawstrings tucked into your slippers are comfortable and do not rub against your skin. If you get a blister, do not try to pop or peel it; keep the skin on the blister. Keep the feet clean to help avoid infecting the blistered area. When dancing, cover the blister with a soft adhesive bandage to avoid irritation. Exposure to air accelerates healing, so outside of class, wear shoes that allow air to get to the blister and at night, leave it uncovered.

Strains

Strains are injuries to muscles or to tendons, which connect muscle to bone. Strains are common dance injuries; they come with the territory of any physical activity. If you have never used a set of muscles or body parts specific to the movement you are learning in ballet class, or if it has been a long time since you have taken a dance class, be prepared to experience some soreness in your body.

To avoid strains while you are learning or practicing new exercises and steps, try to execute movement within your range and know when to stop. Doing too much strenuous exercise or too many repetitions is in line with the adage *no pain, no gain.* However, a better strategy is to slowly increase the number of repetitions and the intensity of the exercise to gain with less pain and more longevity. Beginning students execute most leg extensions at about 45 degrees or lower. Extending a leg to 90 degrees may be a long-term goal, but you should not start there. Start low, then gradually move higher as you gain the strength, flexibility, and control to do the movement.

Sprains

Ankle sprain is the most common injury in ballet. Sprains are injuries to ligaments, which connect bone to bone. Landing on the foot incorrectly from a jump can create a sprain, so pay careful attention to proper landing technique and alignment when jumping. Sprains occur in varying degrees; however, they are more severe than strains and can reoccur if not treated properly. If you endure a sprain, you may notice swelling and bruising in the affected area. To determine the severity of a sprain, treatment options, and the recovery time needed, consult a physician.

Using the PRICED Method

A common treatment for activity-related injuries to the soft tissue such as strains or sprains is the **PRICED** method—**p**rotection, **r**est, **i**ce, **c**ompression, **e**levation, and **d**iagnosis. Your physician might prescribe it to you or you can decide to use it on your own even if your injury is minor. It can be helpful in healing and also in determining the severity of your injury. Use the PRICED method as follows:

- *Protection.* Move away from possible danger.
- *Rest.* Stop dancing so that the injury can heal properly. You must rest so that you can recover before you return to dancing. If you are in severe pain while resting, consult a physician.
- *Ice.* To reduce swelling, which is uncomfortable and can slow healing, place an ice pack on the injured area several times a day. Place the ice on for 20 minutes, then remove it for 20 minutes before placing it on again.
- *Compression.* To help reduce swelling, constrict the injured area by wrapping it with an elastic bandage. Compression does not mean you should wrap it as

tightly as possible; if you feel throbbing, unwrap bandage and wrap it again more loosely.

- ◆ *Elevation.* Raise the injured area above the heart to help reduce swelling.
- ◆ *Diagnosis.* If the injury seems severe, see a health care professional.

Adapted from International Association for Dance Medicine and Science, 2010, *First aid for dancers.*

Warming Up and Stretching

In addition to using correct ballet technique, warming up and stretching properly can help prevent injuries in ballet class. Depending on teacher preference and time constraints, some ballet classes include a pre-barre warm-up and others do not. Doing a personal warm-up can give you time to clear your mind so that you can focus in class. When your mind is focused on the task at hand, you are less prone to accidents. You may need an additional warm-up before the barre because you have had an injury and the affected body part needs extra attention. Or, you may need it because the outside temperature is extremely cold and you need to safely prepare your body for the class; cold muscles are more prone to injuries. In addition, you might want to stretch your muscles to improve flexibility.

Flexibility is desirable for achieving beautiful lines in ballet, but it is also a way to keep the body safe. Flexibility increases your range of motion, causing less strain on the joints when performing dance movements. Some people are naturally flexible while others have to work to gain or maintain flexibility.

Your teacher can help you create a personal warm-up and stretching program, or you can create one based on what you have learned in class. In general, you should begin your warm-up with simple movements in the hips, ankles, and feet, and then slowly start to stretch the legs, spine, and torso. To increase flexibility,

These students are doing personal stretching exercises as part of their ballet class warm-up.

increase your range of motion gradually each time you stretch. Remember, the *no pain, no gain* adage does not apply to stretching. Rather, the reverse is true: Be aware of how your body feels and recognize the difference between discomfort and pain so that you know when to stop.

The basis of good stretching is correct body position, alignment of body parts, and turnout if it is used in the stretch. As with positions and steps, ballet stretches are performed using body directions in relation to personal anatomical points. Using these directional coordinates helps you get the most out of your stretching. Stretching for ballet is a continuous movement, not a ballistic movement. Ballistic movement engages the stretch reflex, which can shorten rather than lengthen the muscles being stretched. Along with any stretching sequence, breathe in conjunction with the movement to deepen and elongate the stretch.

UNDERSTANDING DANCE FITNESS

Ballet is an art form and a physical activity that requires both physical and mental fitness. In ballet class your movements raise your body temperature and you experience a physical workout. While your body works out, your mind prepares you for your next movements, solves problems or records new spatial and kinesthetic information during your execution, and retains a movement memory for you to review and analyze to prepare for the next class. Understanding the relationship between ballet and fitness can help you enhance your performance and your lifestyle with better health.

Principles of Fitness

Principles used in fitness and sports also apply to dance. The **FITT principle**—**f**requency, **i**ntensity, **t**ime, and **t**ype of activity—and the **overload principle** can help in creating an appropriate exercise program that progresses safely. They are described as follows:

- *Frequency.* Most academic ballet classes meet several times a week with usually one day in between. The day or time in between gives your body time to rest and recuperate before undertaking the same type of strenuous activity.

- *Intensity.* This term refers to how hard you exercise during a period of physical activity. As your ballet course progresses, the number and complexity of movements increases to raise the level of intensity.

- *Time.* The duration of each class does not vary, but you can vary the length of time you are active during class and the time you practice outside of class.

- *Type.* Ballet class includes both aerobic and anaerobic activities as well as muscle-building exercises and flexibility work.

- *Overload.* This principle refers to working a targeted muscle group beyond what you have previously done in order to gain strength. The body responds to more difficult demands by adapting itself; depending on the type of overload, it increases strength, endurance, or both.

These fitness principles work together in the dance class. The frequency, intensity, time, and type of exercise affect how the body is overloaded. The body must be given time to create gradual increases in strength and endurance. In addition to regularly attending class, serious dancers include additional conditioning options to support and extend their classwork. The old adage of *if you don't use it, you lose it* applies to dancing in class and conditioning to support your dancing. The dancer is an athlete whose body is the means to meet physical demands to express movement with artistry.

Strength and Conditioning Considerations

As a dancer, you need a strong core of muscles to augment the work you do in ballet class. Sometimes instead of stretching between the barre and the center, dancers engage in push-ups, sit-ups, and other exercises for strength and flexibility. Outside of ballet class, Pilates exercises focus on strengthening the core while keeping the body properly aligned, and weight training can increase muscle strength and help to rehabilitate you from an injury. Doing these and other types of activities can help you increase your general health, enhance your dance performance, and avoid or recover from injury.

NUTRITION, HYDRATION, AND REST

During dance class you use energy to fuel your muscles and your body temperature increases, causing perspiration. Proper nutrition and hydration before, during, and after class help keep your body in peak condition and refuel you for optimal performance and recovery. Beyond good nutrition and hydration, you need adequate rest to physically prepare for and recover from vigorous movement activities and to focus on the mental challenges associated with ballet.

Nutrition

Dancers and nondancers alike should focus on a diet that maintains adequate energy levels throughout the day for overall health. A balanced diet that is rich in fruits and vegetables and includes protein, complex carbohydrates, and fiber helps to support and maintain you for your work in class. To keep you satisfied but not overly full, consume six smaller meals instead of three larger ones each day. Smaller, more frequent meals ensure that you have a constant supply of energy and avoid feeling sluggish during ballet class. Never skip breakfast; it fuels you for starting your day. With each meal, include a protein source, a whole grain, a healthful fat, and fruits and vegetables. Carry healthy snacks with you to replenish energy

DID YOU KNOW?

Rethink your drink: Coffee drinks, soda, alcohol, and sugary beverages may be tempting, but they offer little or no nutrition and can even lead to dehydration. Replacing one or more of these drinks with water during the day will rehydrate you and lower the number of empty calories consumed.

lost during ballet class. To curb those evening snack cravings that everyone faces, eat fruit, whole grain cereal, or popcorn instead of cookies, candy, and other choices with empty calories.

Magazines, websites, and campus health and wellness programs can offer more information on nutrition for dancers and healthy living.

Hydration

Proper hydration is essential before, during, and after dance class and throughout the day. The intensity of ballet class can cause you to lose water through perspiration, so drink water before and after class. During class, drink small amounts of water. After class, you can consume larger quantities. If you choose a sports drink for rehydration, drink it after class, not during class. Drinking a sugared beverage during exercise can cause intestinal cramping.

Rest

To prepare for dance class, you should be well rested. Along with proper nutrition and hydration, adequate rest supports body recovery and revitalization. When muscles are overloaded, they need rest in order to rebuild themselves. Your mind also needs rest for optimal function. When you don't get enough rest, you become less alert and more prone to accidents. If you have trouble sleeping or are too anxious to rest, learn some relaxation techniques and pace yourself during your day so that your body and mind have time to rest.

SUMMARY

Focusing on safety and health helps you to prepare physically and mentally for the rigors of ballet class. Knowing about common injuries in dance can help you prevent and treat them. Understanding the basics of anatomy and kinesiology, fitness principles, and how to take care of your body can give you a new awareness of the physicality of dance and its demands and help you know what to do to make ballet a safe and healthy experience.

To find supplementary materials for this chapter such as learning activities, e-journaling assignments, and web links, visit the web resource at www.HumanKinetics.com/BeginningBallet1E.

Chapter 4

Learning and Performing Ballet Technique

Learning and performing ballet present physical and intellectual challenges; it is the ultimate mind–body experience. You have to come to class mentally and physically ready to learn with your mind open and your body ready. You use your observation skills to see and hear the movements the teacher presents. As you perform the movements, you monitor how well you understand and are able to replicate movement in time to music using appropriate techniques and qualities. These skills are not learned the first week you take ballet; rather, they are acquired over time as your kinesthetic awareness develops. Hence, you repeat exercises and steps but in various patterns and to different music. Repetition of correct movements is what hones your technique and performance. The changing patterns and music expand your ability to deal with new elements in relation to the movements you already know or new steps and exercises that you are learning. Beginning ballet requires learning a new movement language, which includes being able to express yourself well in that language clearly, concisely, and with fluency.

LANGUAGES OF BALLET

Ballet uses several languages with which you must become proficient. The first language you learn is that of ballet movements. To aid you in learning and remembering the movements, **action words** describe body actions, or movements of the legs, arms, and head in a sequence, for an exercise, step, or pose. Learning action words is an intermediate step to learning the French language terms of ballet.

Action Words to French Terms

The teacher uses action words to describe the movement. Saying these words to yourself helps you make a connection to the movement. Then you progress to condensing several actions into an exercise or step. This sequence of movements is represented by a single ballet term for an exercise or step.

When you begin learning ballet, the action words in their sequence cue your movements. Later, you can execute a step or exercise without thinking about each movement, and you can begin to use French ballet terms for the exercises and steps.

DID YOU KNOW?

Ballet developed in the royal court of Louis XIV of France, so terms were expressed in French. Today, ballet is taught around the world and still uses the French language. So, if you were to attend a ballet class in any other country, the teacher would use French ballet terminology.

Spoken and Written Terminology

Understanding ballet terminology goes beyond translating the movement sequence to recognizing either the spoken or written term. Knowing all these translations comes in handy when it comes to exam time; you may be expected to perform the exercise or step, recognize or write the French ballet term, and know its translation into action terms.

The vocabulary of ballet technique includes positions, exercises, steps, and poses. Although the terminology is expressed in the French language, don't confuse ballet French with the French you learn in a language class. The pronunciation of some terms may not be exactly the same. Because ballet French is spoken all over the world, ballet terminology may have a regional accent or even a different pronunciation depending on where you are.

LEARNING BALLET MOVEMENTS

In ballet class students stand quietly and observe while the teacher performs an exercise or combination to music and speaks the action words or ballet terms. Then you execute the movement. Listening and remembering the movement sequence coupled with the action words and their ballet terms help you while practicing the exercise or combination. Learning new ballet movements can be distilled into an easy method: Watch it and hear it, then do it.

Watching

The first step is to watch sequences of movements as the teacher demonstrates them. When you begin to learn ballet, focus on the starting position of the feet, the working leg and its actions, and the directions in which the leg is moving. Later when exercises or steps include arm positions and traveling, you need to view the whole body doing the movement, what each body part is doing in sequence, and where it is in space.

Hearing

While watching the teacher's demonstration, you should also listen to verbal instructions—the cues the teacher uses to describe the movements while executing them. When the music starts, listen to the movement cues spoken in relation to the music. In your beginning practice, the teacher usually cues you just before you start a movement. This is your chance to identify which movement takes place on which count or measure.

As the ballet course progresses, the teacher demonstrates without the action words and instead uses the ballet terminology in rhythm or counts to the music. Near the end of your beginning ballet course, the teacher might say an exercise or combination using ballet terms without including a demonstration of the combination. At this point, you must translate your listening into movement: You have to hear the ballet term, visualize it, and then perform it to the music with the correct rhythm and tempo.

As a beginning dancer, translating the teacher's words into movement is your ultimate goal for learning terminology. While you move from one phase of listening to translating, you likewise gain control of and responsibility for your movement.

Doing

The next step is to do the movement. When learning a new movement sequence, you usually execute the movements slowly without music, then slowly with music, while the teacher guides you from one movement to the next. As you practice the movement sequence, visualize it and say the action words or terms to yourself. Continue to fit the movements in their proper sequence and in time to the music, then practice the movement sequence until you become comfortable with it. Be prepared to make adjustments in order to perform the movement correctly. Remember, at this time you are learning just the basic movement patterns.

During the course, you begin to think about how technique, principles, rules, and other elements will refine your performance of beginning exercises. In ballet, refining your movement is an unceasing process. After you have the movement sequence in mind, practice it so that both sides of the body can initiate it.

As a beginning dancer, make it a goal to absorb most of the movement presented in class. In some classes, some or many of the components are repeated during the next class meeting. This repetition reinforces learning. In ballet, you have to attain a certain level of learning before you can progress to the next level of technique,

Repeatedly practicing steps at the barre, in the center, and outside of class reinforces learning and helps perfect technique.

style, and artistry. Your ability to remember and replicate movement contributes to your progress as a dancer.

LEARNING BALLET TECHNIQUE

The beginning ballet class is all about learning basic **technique**, or how to perform a specific exercise and step in a consistent manner. Technique involves correct performance but also incorporation of movement principles that apply to the exercise or step in a combination. Beyond learning technique, the dancer adds timing and quality to movement to develop clarity in performance, which leads to an awareness of conveying style and which radiates musicality and artistry.

Using Cues and Feedback

During class, several strands of feedback can guide your development as a performer. The teacher provides you with cues in various forms as you learn new movement. Cues might be in the form of instructions or imagery to help you sense the movement, or they could be rhythmic phrasing or counts indicating the timing of a step. These are just a few types of the many cues the teacher may use.

Most often the teacher's feedback is directed to the beginning class to help all students understand the movement or sequence. Sometimes, the teacher gives individual feedback to clarify or extend a specific student's performance. Individual feedback becomes more common during the latter part of the class.

Another type of feedback comes from your personal performance. This feedback can be kinesthetic, intellectual, or a combination. When you execute a movement, you feel how your body is moving and applying movement principles throughout a sequence. While doing the movement, you mentally track the movement timing with the music and the kinesthetic sense of doing the movement, record the experience in your movement memory, and prepare for the next movement—all at the same time. With practice over time, these processes blend to the point where you can be responsible for fine-tuning your performance of the movement.

Putting Movements in Context

Knowing the parts of a movement sequence and timing for a step later extends to several steps as a combination. An introductory step, one or more middle steps, and an ending step form a basic combination. Each step in the combination requires clear execution with specific timing and quality.

Sensing Directions

Steps in a combination can move in a variety of directions: forward, backward, to the side, or on a diagonal. Gaining a sense of direction in ballet requires precision. Directions relate to anatomical points on the body and to the studio or performance area.

The first step in learning directions is to locate anatomical body points in relation to front, side, and back. To find these points, you must know where your **center line** is (see figure 4.1). If you were to draw a vertical line down the front midpoint of your body, it would divide into two halves. The arm or leg on one side of the body complements the other arm or leg in symmetrical or asymmetrical designs created through positions, poses, exercises, or steps.

At the barre, exercises that focus on leg and foot movements move front, side, and back in direct lines, angular patterns, or circular patterns. These exercises help you acquire directional acuity. Directions are an integral part of ballet technique. Chapter 5 covers directions in more detail.

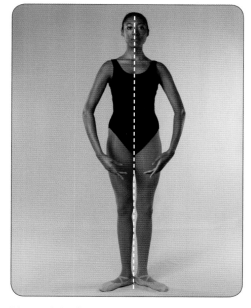

Another sense of direction is body movement in space. When the body moves forward, backward, or to either side in space while executing steps or a combination, these actions become more complicated. In addition to moving in different directions horizontally, you should be confident in moving downward by bending your knees, rising, or jumping into the air. Some exercises or steps require that you remain **sur la place**, or stay in one place, during a sequence that moves up or down within the space.

Body Directions

In classical ballet, body directions include facing front or to the corners of the performance area. These body directions to the corners use

Figure 4.1 Center line of the body.

ACTIVITY ▷▷▷▷▷▷▷▷▷▷

Finding Directions

Facing a mirror, raise an arm to the front, to the side, and then to the back. Then, do the same action with a leg. See and sense each specific directional path made by your arm or leg actions, then repeat the exercise facing away from the mirror. When you feel you have a kinesthetic sense of these directions, ask another student to watch you perform them and give feedback about your performance.

crossed or open positions and extend into a series of classical positions that are part of poses or movements. As a beginning dancer, you learn these classical positions as poses so that you can understand their distinct lines. As you advance in your ballet studies, the classical positions interface with movements and steps. Chapter 5 and the web resource cover classical body directions in depth.

Stage Directions

Stage directions relate to the walls and corners of the dance space, which could be the dance studio or another performance space such as a stage. Stage directions give performers a spatial awareness for moving in relation to the performance space. Start by standing in the center of the studio facing the mirror or front wall, which is similar to facing the audience. The front of the studio is downstage, where the audience would sit in the auditorium or house, and behind you is upstage. From the center of the studio, on your right is stage right and on your left is stage left.

Stage directions for dancers are sequentially numbered using one of two numbering systems, depending on whether you are studying the Russian method or the Cecchetti method (figure 4.2). Russian stage directions begin at center front, then sequentially number the corners and walls of the dance space in a clockwise direction. Cecchetti stage directions begin at numbering the corners of the dance space, starting with the right downstage corner and moving counterclockwise, followed by center front, or the audience, and the walls in a counterclockwise direction. **Dancer stage directions** give performers a spatial awareness for moving in relation to the studio space in preparation for dancing on stage.

Your teacher will determine which set of dance stage directions to use in class. Knowing the numbering systems helps dancers gain a sense of the directions the body faces during combinations in a specific space.

Memorizing Movement Sequences

As you gain experience in ballet, the teacher eventually stops cuing your movements and you become responsible for remembering movement

DID YOU KNOW?

The terms *downstage* and *upstage* originated during a time when theater stages were raked, or slanted. In the 18th century, a **raked stage** slanted upward away from the audience, allowing the audience members seated on a level floor to see the performers better. Dancing on a raked stage presented challenges for dancers, especially since they performed in high heels.

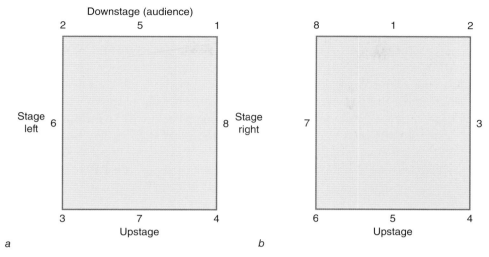

Figure 4.2 *(a)* Cecchetti stage directions. 1: right front corner, or downstage right; 2: left front corner, or downstage left; 3: left back corner, or upstage left; 4: right back corner, or upstage right; 5: front (en face), or facing the audience; 6: left wall, or stage left; 7: back wall, or upstage; 8: right wall, or stage right. *(b)* Russian stage directions.

sequences. So, you must either memorize the terminology or create your own terms for the movements and repeat them to yourself as you dance. In addition, ask yourself questions such as these:

- Which direction am I facing?
- Which leg is moving?
- In which direction is the leg moving?
- What is the position of my arms?
- In which direction is my body moving?

Repeating action words or the teacher's cues to yourself as you move helps you memorize movement. Once you can perform the movement sequence, try to execute it without saying the words so that you can associate the entire movement sequence with the French ballet term. Learning this technique of self-talk in the beginning can help you integrate other elements such as technique and movement principles in time to the music. Self-talk continues to expand as exercises and combinations get longer and more complicated.

Connecting to Your Kinesthetic Sense

Connecting to your kinesthetic sense requires awareness of your body in space and its movement. Making this connection takes time and experience; it does not happen overnight. After you have practiced ballet consistently with awareness for a while, your kinesthetic sense becomes part of the translation process in the language–movement connection; when you hear a French ballet term, your body just knows what to do and how to do it.

Movement Memory

Movement memory covers information presented in the beginning ballet class from the past, connecting it to the present and the future. Movements you perform in class are based on movement memory, also called muscle memory, which connects to developing your kinesthetic sense. This type of memory incorporates continued feedback to the basic movement to clarify the sequence of the legs or alter the arms and head in an exercise or step. Later, movement memory expands as exercises and combinations get longer, contain more steps, and increasingly become more complex. After practicing many repetitions of a movement, you can execute the movement without thinking of the different parts, yet you are able to apply feedback or add stylistic elements to enhance the movement into a more sophisticated performance.

Movement Vocabulary

As you continue to take classes, you gain a foundational movement vocabulary of ballet exercises, steps, positions, and poses. You record your movement vocabulary in a variety of ways: kinesthetic, visual, auditory, and as rhythmic components. You use both movement and action words, which link to a ballet term.

Transposing Movement

To perform ballet, you must be able to execute exercises and steps on both sides of the body, or transpose movement. Although one side of your body may respond more easily than the other, the goal is to be able to execute the movement equally well on both sides.

When you exercise at the barre, the tradition is to stand with your left hand on the barre and begin with the right foot, which is the outside foot. Following the execution of the exercise, you turn toward the barre to face the other side with the right hand on the barre and the left foot as the outside foot, then perform the exercise to the other side. In the center, the tradition is to stand with the right foot forward in position to execute the combination with the right foot. Then, you perform the combination again beginning with the left foot. When you perform combinations, you move from one direction to another direction. Sometimes a combination moves from side to side, front to back, or back to front. In some parts of the class, you may move across the floor in straight lines or on a diagonal from a back corner of the room to an opposite front corner. Some steps require that you turn or do some circular movements. Learning to transpose exercises and steps from one foot or side to the other helps to prepare you for moving in various directions.

Mental Practice

Mental practice enhances physical performance. Mental practice is similar to learning by watching, hearing, and doing. Using this technique, you visualize perfectly performing the movements to the music. When you review ballet terminology during mental practice, it can support making a movement–language connection, too.

Gaining a Performance Attitude

Gaining a **performance attitude** means that you learn to think, act, and move like a dancer. The first step to gaining a performance attitude is to be able to perform a movement sequence and transpose it to the other side. Once you can memorize a movement and transpose it independently without relying on your teacher, you become responsible for your own movement. Then your teacher can

ACTIVITY ▶ ▶ ▶ ▶ ▶ ▶ ▶ ▶ ▶ ▶

Meet Your Ballet Muse

Imagine stepping into the shoes of a dancer: You are observing, moving, thinking, and feeling like a dancer. When you stand at the barre or in the center, construct a visual image of a dancer performing the movement correctly in front of you so that you can follow that dancer while you perform the movement.

build on your learning in the next class. As you gain movement confidence, you develop a performance attitude and build performance confidence. Acquiring performance confidence comes over time and with the experience of executing combinations within your growing dance vocabulary.

UNDERSTANDING MUSICALITY

Musicality is knowledge about and sensitivity to music. In dance, it refers to how the dancer executes movement in relation to music. Executing movement that is technically correct and in time to the music is the baseline of performance. As you progress, you not only dance in time to the music but also use the music to express the qualities of both the movement and music to understand musicality.

Dancing to the Music

Ballet exercises, steps, and combinations are danced in time with the music. Knowing basic time signatures, hearing the beat, and determining note values are underlying factors for developing movement qualities and musicality.

The time signatures of music usually used in a beginning ballet class include:

- ◆ *4/4 or 2/4*. In 4/4 time, there are four beats to each measure of music. In 2/4 time, there are two beats to each measure. Both time signatures are used in exercises at the barre and during the petit allegro and other combinations in the center.

- ◆ *3/4*. In 3/4 time, also known as waltz time, there are three beats to each measure. This time signature supports a variety of exercises at the barre and during adagio, and some petit to grand allegro combinations in the center.

Listening to the music provides musical cues for hearing the notes, measures, phrases, and structure of the music that accompanies the movement.

Counting Music

Dancers count by measures. When executing a barre exercise, the teacher may specify either one or two measures for each exercise or step. Sometimes, movements

The musician for dance supports beginning dancers' understanding of music and their development of musicality.

are executed twice as slowly in either half time or cut time. This allows you time to think about and learn all of the parts of the movement and their sequence.

In class, you should anticipate the music rather than react to it. This difference shows up in your dancing. You have to accent certain movements and complete them on time with the music so that you achieve a synergy with the music instead of appear to be dragged by it. Two general tempos depict ballet exercises and combinations. **Adagio** refers to moving slowly to music. An adagio step can extend over several measures. As your experience level increases, adagio combinations expand the measures because of the slow movements. **Allegro** refers to moving to a fast or brisk tempo. Allegro tempos increase as combinations become more complex.

Timing and Quality in Performance

Associated with knowing the exercise or step is its timing and quality of performance. Determine whether the movement performed is a slow step or a fast step. Recognize if the movement has a gliding quality or a sharp, striking quality to mirror or contrast the music. As part of the ballet class, you practice dancing to various types of music, at varying tempos and time signatures. Likewise, you practice various steps that make up combinations of different or perhaps similar qualities. Learning to identify these and other characteristics of the combination eventually becomes second nature; however, in the beginning class, identifying these characteristics is part of learning basic ballet technique. In early beginning ballet classes, the tempo of exercises and steps is slow to ensure that your mind and your body understand each movement and the sequence. In steps and combinations across the floor, moving slowly and filling out the music with jumps and leaps help you acquire both the power and height you will need for when the music tempo gets faster.

UNDERSTANDING ARTISTRY

In dance, **artistry** means being able to express the intent of the dance, the choreographer's ideas, and emotions through ballet movements and gestures with the music. Similar to reading a great poem, seeing a riveting dramatic performance, listening to a piece of music that transports your spirit, or viewing a work of art that connects to your senses, a dance artist visually expresses through the fullness and elegance of movements and gestures in relation with the music that accompanies the performance—the poetry, emotion, and drama of dance. This is what you see on stage when a dance artist interprets a choreographic work or a dramatic role in a ballet. Developing artistry is not studied separately from technique, nor is it studied only in advanced classes. Actually, it starts in the beginning ballet classes.

Every day as you perform in ballet class, the exercises and steps are parts of a bigger picture of studying ballet as an art form. While you perform beginning ballet combinations, you learn to apply techniques, movement principles, rules, and protocols. These fundamentals underlie aesthetics and performance artistry.

APPLYING AESTHETIC PRINCIPLES TO BALLET

All dance forms share the same aesthetic principles that underlie the arts and function as a basis by which choreographers, dancers, and the audience judge a dance work. In the dance studio, the aesthetic principles as they apply to ballet guide the teacher in developing combinations. Students learn to understand and practice applying these principles through performing ballet combinations.

The general aesthetic principles that underlie other art forms and dance are shown in figure 4.3. They include the following:

- *Unity* is cohesion of all the elements of a combination that make it a whole statement.

- *Variety* refers to steps, directions, and levels that keep and hold the attention or even challenge the dancer.

- *Contrast* highlights or stimulates interest and adds dimensions to the dance.

- *Repetition* is the repeated occurrence of an element that makes it a constant.

- *Balance* provides a sense of proportion to the combination that gives it a sense of equality between the parts.

Adapted, by permission, from G. Kassing and D. Jay, 2003, *Dance teaching methods and curriculum design* (Champaign, IL: Human Kinetics), 121.

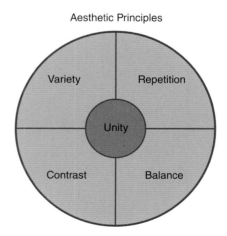

Figure 4.3 Aesthetic principles support dance and other art forms.

These aesthetic principles may seem abstract and disconnected to the movements and steps that constitute beginning ballet and its technique. However, after you acquire a working vocabulary of ballet and understand movement principles and rules, aesthetic principles come into play so that ballet expands beyond being a technical art and becomes an expressive one as well. In order for this connection to become integrated into your performance, you have to gain awareness of the aesthetic principles and how they relate to ballet. Integrating the aesthetic principles into your dancing begins with performing ballet as an artist from day 1 in the ballet class. When you practice movement principles, rules, and protocols so that they become integrated into your performance, you lay a foundation upon which you can layer qualities, style, musicality, and personal interpretation. This is a continuous synergy and development that deepens over time, with practice, and with concerted attention to your physical and mental understanding of ballet.

PREPARING FOR CLASS PERFORMANCE TESTING

In an academic ballet class, you take two types of tests: written (either on paper or online) and performance. The written test covers vocabulary, action terms, French ballet terminology, ballet principles, rules, and protocols. The performance test involves the class performing exercises at the barre and combinations in the center. In addition, you may be expected to write journals or e-journals, response papers, and dance performance reviews.

Generally to expedite performance tests, the entire class performs barre and center combinations for one or two class periods. Usually you learn and practice the combinations in class and memorize them for performing with your class or group.

On the day of the performance test, your teacher presents barre and center combinations and expects you to execute them from memory. You should practice to ensure that you have the movement sequence and technique correct, you coordinate your movements with the music, and you express the quality of the combination. Use practice strategies to prepare for your test in and out of class. The following questions help you remember combinations at the barre and in the center.

- What direction do I face to start?
- What is the starting foot position?
- What is the preparation (foot and arms)?
- What is the first movement?
- What is the sequence of the combination?
- What is the ending?

With practice and experience, answering these questions becomes second nature and they function as self-check points in your performance.

Practicing for the Performance Test

To prepare for the performance test, practice the required combinations. These movements become deeply embedded in your movement and intellectual memory. The following steps help you acquire this level of understanding.

1. Practice each of the combinations by yourself until you feel confident.
2. Execute the combinations facing the mirror while you do a self-check for correctness.
3. Practice the combinations facing away from the mirror and do a self-check.
4. Make a list of the combinations you feel confident about and those that require some extra study. Then focus your practice on the specific areas that need attention.
5. Practice the combinations with a partner observing you, then observe your partner. Share feedback on each other's execution and share areas to review.

In a performance test, you must know and be able to perform all the combinations of the performance test. Often during class and performance testing, students follow people in front of them or watch them in the mirror. This practice is detrimental; it confirms for the teacher that you either cannot perform the combination without outside visual help or you have not accepted your responsibility for knowing and performing the combinations.

Between class practices of the test, review the test by mentally visualizing yourself performing and by physically practicing the combinations. Before the performance test, make time to do a mental review of the test combinations. During the performance test, you have to think about the movement you are executing and also think ahead to transitions and to the next movements in the combination.

To perform each movement in the combination you have to do all parts of it from start to finish fully and with the correct energy level and dynamics. Even if you have prepared for the test and have confidence that you know the combinations, problems can surface during performance. Keep a mindset that if you should encounter a problem or make a mistake, you will keep your performance attitude and complete the combination. Also, keep these ideas in mind:

- Think in the moment and think ahead.
- Deal with problems, recover, and then focus your attention on the next movement.
- Complete every movement.
- Finish the combination.

Waiting to Perform

While you are standing quietly at either the back or side of the studio for your group to perform the next combination, you have an opportunity to mentally and physically review the next combination. If it is distracting for other groups to perform, then just turn away from the performance taking place, stand quietly, and mentally review the sequence of the next combination. In some classes **marking**, or moving through, the steps of the current or next combination may be considered discourteous. Instead, train yourself to visualize your performance with correct technique, rhythm, timing, and dynamics to the music as it plays. Your teacher will indicate rules about student expectations and use of marking during a performance test.

Reflecting After the Performance Test

After the performance test, take time to reflect on the combinations and your personal performance. Understanding what you did well can help you build on strengths. Identifying areas that need additional work can give you goals to think about in future classes.

SUMMARY

Beginning ballet focuses on learning and performing basic ballet technique. At first you learn to understand and express the movement vocabulary in action words and then in French terminology through spoken and written forms. Learning to perform ballet is an integrated art experience involving your body and mind. From day 1 of ballet class, understanding musicality and artistry, applying aesthetic principles, and acquiring a performance attitude are other goals. Testing helps you find out which performance goals you have met and which ones need work; it is part of the process of learning and performing beginning ballet technique.

To find supplementary materials for this chapter such as learning activities, e-journaling assignments, and web links, visit the web resource at www.HumanKinetics.com/BeginningBallet1E.

5

Basics of Ballet Technique

Several characteristics distinguish ballet technique from that of other dance genres. These characteristics include specific foot and arm positions that are unique to ballet. Underlying ballet technique is a series of movement principles that support and interrelate with one another through exercises and combinations. Stage directions, body facings, and leg, foot, and arm directions create the three-dimensionality of poses and movement. Patterns and types of combinations at the barre and in the center outline structures for practice, which contributes to movement experience and fluency of technique. Together these elements define ballet technique, structure, and aesthetics.

In the beginning ballet class you usually learn basic foot and arm positions and some that represent a specific school or method of ballet. This chapter presents positions and directions. Your teacher determines whether a specific method will be applied to basic ballet technique. The Cecchetti method and the Russian method are specified in some of the foot positions in this chapter.

DID YOU KNOW? ⟩⟩⟩⟩⟩⟩⟩⟩⟩   ▶▶▶

Classical ballet developed various schools, methods, and styles over the 19th and 20th centuries. Near the end of the 19th century Enrico Cecchetti, a dancer and teacher in the Italian tradition, brought his expertise to the imperial theaters of Russia. In the 20th century, the Cecchetti method of teaching was codified in his writings. Today, teachers and organizations carry on Cecchetti's method of teaching ballet.

In the early part of the 20th century, Agrippina Vaganova (1879-1951), a Russian ballerina and renowned teacher, formulated the Vaganova method. Later, Russian dancers and teachers spread these approaches as they performed and settled throughout the world.

The Cecchetti method, Vaganova, and Russian methods are three of several major ballet styles. During the 20th century, other styles emerged from major ballet teachers and choreographers across the world. With the proliferation of ballet programs in academic settings, various ballet styles blended.

POSITIONS OF THE FEET

Ballet technique is based on five basic positions of the feet. In these positions, the weight of the body is vertically centered over the feet. Figures 5.1 through 5.5 show the five positions of the feet.

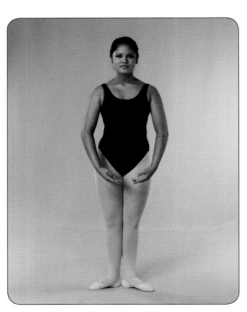

Figure 5.1   First position: The heels of the feet touch and both legs are equally turned out.

Full-Foot Position

In a **full-foot position** the entire foot is on the floor, such as in the five foot positions shown in figures 5.1 through 5.5. Each toe extends on the floor, especially the fifth toe. When the entire sole of the foot is on the floor, three major points are in contact with the floor to create a **foot triangle** (figure 5.6). These three points are the first metatarsal (under the big toe), the fifth metatarsal (between the fourth and fifth toes), and the center of the heel. If you connect these points, they form a triangle. The dancer places the weight over the center of this triangle to connect to the vertical alignment of the body.

Along with the toes, the foot triangle supports your weight evenly. Maintaining the foot triangle in full-foot position is a key part of your alignment, turnout, and stance in foot positions or weight transference when you execute exercises or combinations.

Figure 5.2 Second position: The feet are separated about the distance of one and one half of the dancer's foot length, up to shoulder-width apart. Both great toes are on a straight line to ensure equal turnout.

Figure 5.3 Third position: The heel of the front foot touches the middle of the arch of the back foot.

Figure 5.4 Fourth position: The distance between the back and the front foot is the length of one of the dancer's feet. For the beginning dancer, fourth position can be forward of either *(a)* first position or *(b)* third position.

Figure 5.5 Fifth position: The heel of the front foot touches the back foot. *(a)* In the Russian method, the heel touches the tip of the toe of the back foot. *(b)* In the Cecchetti method, the heel touches the back foot at the joint of the great toe.

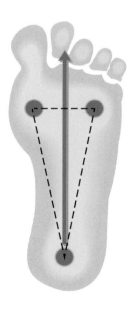

Figure 5.6 Foot triangle.

Finding Your Foot Triangle

Try each position of the feet and think about your foot triangle on each foot. Practice finding the foot triangle in first, second, and third positions. Repeat the foot positions again, using your kinesthetic sense to locate your foot triangle in each position. Then, practice first through fifth positions and find the foot triangle in each position. For third, fourth, and fifth positions, practice first with one foot in front and then with the other foot in front.

Working Foot and Supporting Foot

In ballet, either foot may assume a supporting role or a working role. The **supporting foot** supports the weight of the body. The **working foot** points in various directions on the floor, in the air, or resting on the supporting leg.

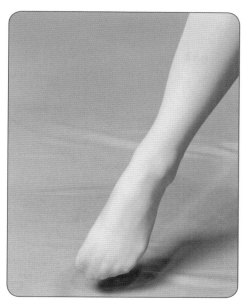
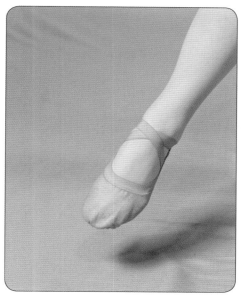

Pointed foot in the air.

Pointing the Foot

The pointed foot is a hallmark of ballet; it is a technical and aesthetic requirement of this art form. In ballet, **pointing** the foot begins at the ankle, by stretching and lifting the arch to point the entire foot from the heel through the lower foot, metatarsals, and toes. The pointed foot continues the straight line of the lower leg. When the foot points, the toes stretch straight without tension to lengthen the line of the foot. On the floor, only the tips of the toes touch the floor. Pointing the foot has a practical benefit, too: The stretched, pointed foot in the air prepares you to articulate through the foot into a smooth landing from a jump or hop.

ACTIVITY

Rehearsing the Five Positions of the Feet

Repeat each foot position, finding the foot triangle on both feet. Between each position, point the right foot to the side and close it in the next position in the sequence. Do this exercise from first position through third position. Repeat the exercise from first position through fifth position. When changing from third position to fourth position, point the right foot, stretch it forward, and press in fourth position. When moving from fourth to fifth position, point the foot and then draw it back into fifth position. Complete this exercise with the right foot as the working foot, then repeat it with the left foot as the working foot.

Active-Foot Position

In an **active-foot position,** one foot supports the weight of the body while the other foot assumes an active, pointed position on the floor, in the air, or resting on the supporting leg. Active-foot positions are listed and pictured in chapter 6.

POSITIONS OF THE ARMS AND PORT DE BRAS

In ballet, the arms describe the space around the body as they move. Positions of the arms complement classic positions of the feet, positions of the body, and movement. In classical ballet, arms create long, curved lines with the elbows out to the sides. To achieve this line, the arm slightly flexes at the elbow and the wrist. The hand extends the line of the arm. For many classical ballet positions, the arms and hands are positioned in front of the body. For some classical ballet poses, the arms and hands extend in long, straight lines rather than in curved positions. The arms in ballet complement the exercises or steps being performed.

Coordinating the arms with foot and leg movements requires time and patience to integrate. Executing positions of the arms in a sequence requires the interplay of movement coupled with breath.

Arm Positions

Classical ballet has five basic positions of the arms. They are numbered similar to positions of the feet. Positions of the arms include variations, based on the ballet method.

Preparatory position (similar to fifth position en bas): In this position, the arms stretch down in front of the body with the sides of the little fingers almost but not touching the body (figure 5.7). Ballet teachers often tell students to imagine holding an apple in each palm.

First position: The arms stretch in front of the body parallel to the bottom of the sternum or higher, forming an oval shape. The hands are slightly separated (figure 5.8).

Second position: Arms stretch to the sides of the body (à la seconde) either just below shoulder height (Russian) or sloping downward and slightly rounded (Cecchetti) (figure 5.9).

Demi-seconde (half-second) position: The arms stretch at half the height between second position and fifth position en bas (figure 5.10).

Third position: One arm is high overhead, while the other arm stretches in second position. If the right foot is front in third position, then the right arm is overhead (figure 5.11).

Fourth position: One arm is high overhead, while the other arm curves in front of the waistline (figure 5.12a). If the right foot is front in fourth position, the right arm is high.

Figure 5.7 Preparatory position.

Figure 5.8 First position.

(a)

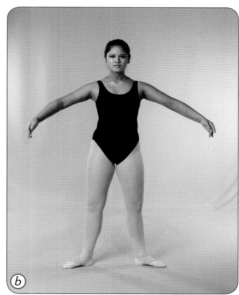

(b)

Figure 5.9 Second position: *(a)* Russian method; *(b)* Cecchetti method.

Fourth position en avant (in front): One arm curves in front at the waistline and the other arm stretches in second position. If the right foot is front in fourth position, the left arm curves in front of the waistline (figure 5.12*b*).

Fifth position en haut (high): Both arms rise high overhead (figure 5.13). The arms are diagonally upward from the hairline (Cecchetti method) or over

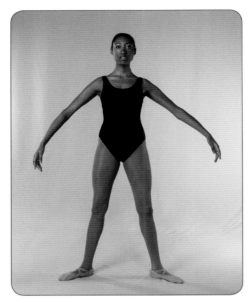

Figure 5.10 Demi-seconde position.

Figure 5.11 Third position.

Figure 5.12 *(a)* Fourth position; *(b)* fourth position en avant.

the crown of the head (Russian method). Since ballet methods have different distinct placement of the arms, your teacher can specify any distinct arm placement.

Figure 5.13 Fifth position: *(a)* Russian, *(b)* Cecchetti.

Port de Bras

Carriage of the arms, or **port de bras,** has several meanings. For port de bras you use the entire arm and hand as a unit to move to and through a position. Port de bras can mean simply moving your arms through a position when performing an exercise. Before each exercise and combination, a port de bras serves as an introduction to your performance. Port de bras can be the name of a section of the center work in which you combine several arm movements into a sequence. For the beginning ballet class, there are two basic port de bras.

▶ First Port de Bras

To execute a first port de bras, begin with the arms in the preparatory position, or fifth position en bas. Raise the arms to the sternum with the fingers almost touching. Then, open both arms to second position. In one version you stop with the arms in second position; in another, you return the arms to the preparatory position. If you perform the latter version, before returning the arms to the preparatory position, slightly rotate the upper arms and elbows, then flex the wrists as the arms float down to the preparatory position.

At the beginning level of performing ballet, often the arm movement stays in a specific position such as second position or the preparatory position following the port de bras. This enables you to first concentrate on the footwork without the complication of adding arm movements. It also serves as a way to learn to hold your arms in a specific position without tensing them for the duration of an exercise.

▶ Second Port de Bras

To perform a second port de bras, begin in preparatory position, or fifth position en bas. Raise both arms to fifth position en haut. There, rotate the arms outward and lower them down to second position. Then lift the elbows slightly and float the arms downward, finishing in preparatory position.

The smooth, continuous, coordinated arm movements of the port de bras can complement or counterpoint the leg and foot movements in an exercise or combination.

Practicing first and second port de bras is the basis for incorporating port de bras into the preparation for barre and center work. Later, arm positions are incorporated into the exercises or arms are held in a specific position until the end of the exercise or combination.

MOVEMENT PRINCIPLES FOR BALLET

Like all dance forms, ballet relies on a set of movement principles. One or more of the principles interface with poses through exercises, steps, and combinations. **Movement principles** incorporate scientific and aesthetic concepts into ballet technique. Understanding each principle and how to apply it is part of learning ballet technique.

Looking at the movement principles pyramid shown in figure 5.14, begin at the bottom tier. As your technique increases, you move upward from the bottom tier, which includes the basic principles of alignment, turnout, and stance. The second level of the pyramid comprises distribution of weight and transfer of weight. Moving up the pyramid, squareness is the central principle and relates to lift (also known as pull-up) and counterpull. Counterbalance and aplomb form the next level, and although balance is at the tip of the pyramid, it is the movement principle that connects all of the tiers.

Alignment

Having proper **alignment** means having good posture that integrates the dancer's body as a whole—head, torso, arms, and legs. Alignment is both a static and a dynamic movement principle, which means it applies when holding a pose (static) and while the body moves through space (dynamic). Dancers adjust body alignment quickly and with control during exercises and combinations. Once one part the body is out of align-

---

ACTIVITY ▶ ▶ ▶ ▶ ▶ ▶ ▶ ▶ ▶ ▶

Assessing Your Alignment

Developing good alignment leads to efficient movement and is a healthy living habit. To help you establish and maintain good alignment habits, think about alignment and do self-checks as you go through your daily routine. Check how you stand or walk at different times of the day and in various situations. Just doing three to five checks a day alerts you about your alignment and reminds you to think about alignment as you walk or stand. Go to the web resource to complete the Assessing Your Alignment activity.

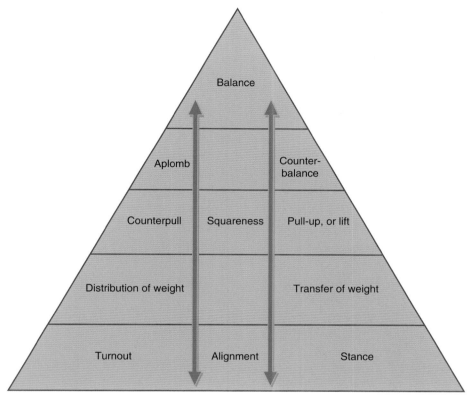

Figure 5.14 Pyramid of movement principles of classical ballet.

ment, other parts compensate, causing misalignment and possible injury. When the body is not aligned it affects all major joints. Learning and practicing good alignment are critical to correct dancing and benefit you both inside and out of class.

Turnout

The hallmark of ballet technique is turnout, the outward rotation of the legs and feet that begins in the hip socket. Deep rotator muscles around the hip support the ability of the leg to rotate in the hip socket. Turnout extends from the hip joint through the upper and lower leg and the foot. Muscles of the upper and lower legs and the abdominal muscles are essential to attaining and controlling turnout.

As a beginning dancer, the angle of your turnout should be at natural turnout, which is about 90 degrees, or 45 degrees for each leg. As you practice turnout, your legs and feet gain muscle memory to stand, move, and stop while continuing to maintain the turnout in various positions.

Stance

When you stand or move, the weight of your body is either on both feet or one foot. In classical ballet **stance**, the weight on both feet should be equally

ACTIVITY ▶▶▶▶▶▶▶▶▶▶

Thinking About Your Turnout

Visualize the turnout of each leg as it spirals down the leg and foot. Use this image as you take various foot positions or move through exercises.

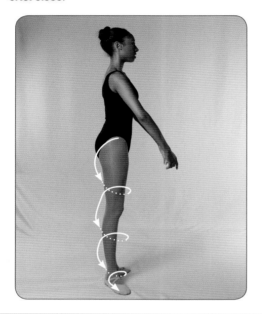

Squareness

Squareness is the central movement principle in the third tier of the pyramid of principles. In ballet, the torso works as a unit, so the shoulders and hips should be level and face the same direction. Using the squareness principle, the torso is quiet and square, which allows focus on leg movements and their directions or on entire body movements in relation to the dance space (figure 5.16). In the beginning ballet class, you first perform barre exercises facing the barre so that you can understand and practice this principle. In the center, squareness

distributed over the foot triangle. Stance has an obvious connection to alignment. Weight distribution and weight transfer interact directly with stance.

Weight Distribution and Weight Transfer

Standing poised and ready to move from two feet to one or from one foot to two initially requires thought behind the movement. You have to know where your weight is (**weight distribution**; on both feet or one foot) and to where it is going (**weight transfer**; to the same foot, other foot, or both feet) as you stand or move. Good alignment has a direct connection to weight distribution through the feet. Consequently, weight distribution connects to your turnout, too. Together the principles of weight distribution, transfer, turnout, and alignment link to stance and ultimately to the foot triangle (figure 5.15).

ACTIVITY ▶▶▶▶▶▶▶▶▶▶▶▶▶▶▶▶▶▶

Squareness

Picture a dot on each shoulder and the front of each hip bone. Then try to line up the dots on the same plane.

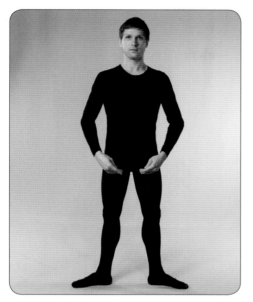 

Figure 5.15 Stance: *(a)* both feet; *(b)* one foot.

applies to using body directions in relation to the space.

Pull-Up, or Lift

As a dancer, whether you are standing or moving you stretch upward from the floor. The principle of **pull-up**, or **lift**, is a combination of connecting the body to the floor while stretching the legs upward from the floor, engaging the abdominals and extending upward to lengthen the torso between the hips and the ribs (figure 5.17). A complete energy line runs as a circuit down the back and up the front of the body. Creating this image of an energy circuit enables you to engage the entire body in relation to the floor in exercises, steps, positions, and poses.

While executing an exercise at the barre, the supporting leg uses pull-up, or lift, to keep the body from sinking or sitting into the supporting leg. Stretching the supporting leg allows

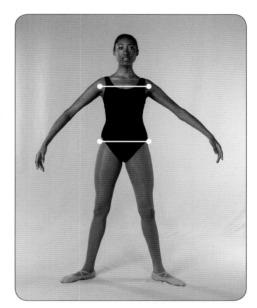

Figure 5.16 Squareness.

the working foot to close completely in fifth position. While moving, applying the principle of pull-up, or lift, gives you the appearance of floating or gliding above the floor. In steps with the working leg extended in the air, pull up the supporting leg and engage the abdominal muscles to stretch the body upward and give the appearance of lifting. Pull-up, or lift, poises the body to move or jump. In small

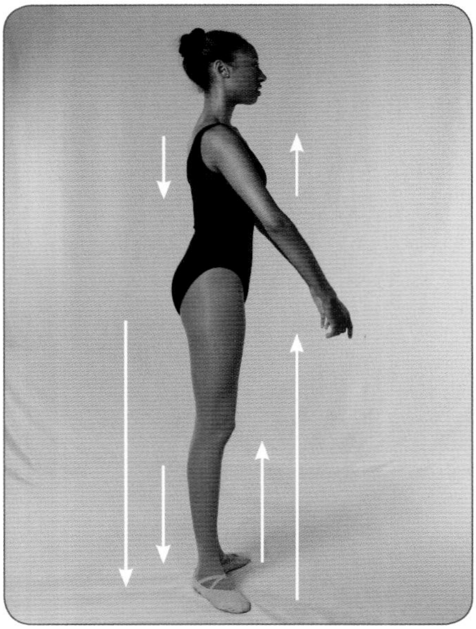

Figure 5.17 Lift, also known as pull-up.

ACTIVITY

Practicing Pull-Up, or Lift

To gain a sense of pull-up, or lift, stand in first position and place your hands on either side of your waist to help you stretch upward, but not off the floor. This feeling of being supported and almost suspended is similar to the principles of pull-up, or lift. Try to transfer this sense of pull-up when executing an exercise or step.

and large jumping movements, lift adds to your elevation. When you use the mental image of pulling up and lifting, you stretch the body vertically, move the legs and feet with ease, and appear to defy gravity, demonstrating desirable aesthetic qualities of ballet.

Counterpull

When the body descends, either from a jump to the floor or when executing a descending movement such as a grand plié, **counterpull** is the oppositional lift that prevents the body from giving in to gravity. Like pull-up or lift, this principle uses a mental image of stretching upward. Counterpull is another movement principle that contributes to the ballet aesthetic of defying gravity.

Counterbalance

When performing a leg extension to the back, the back moves into a position that counterbalances the weight of the leg. Using **counterbalance**, the torso tilts upward, stretching on a slightly forward angle when the working leg lifts beyond 20 degrees to the back (figure 5.18). Not all ballet technique methods use the principle of counterbalance.

Aplomb

The ability to appear to move vertically either upward or downward is **aplomb**. As a ballet dancer you learn to move horizontally and vertically with ease. The movement principle of aplomb links directly to alignment and subsequently to weight distribution and transfer, lift, and other principles.

Balance

At the apex of the pyramid, **balance** is the principle that the dancer uses to continually readjust the alignment of body parts to one another in a pose or while

Figure 5.18 Counterbalance.

moving. Balance is a dynamic principle that relates to each of the other principles in the pyramid, especially to alignment.

Movement principles underlie the development of a sound ballet technique. In a beginning ballet class you have many things to think about. Constant awareness of what principles to incorporate into the pose or movement helps your performance develop technically and aesthetically. These are the first steps for developing a foundation of ballet as a performing art form.

DIRECTIONS OF THE BODY

Directions of the body are an integral part of ballet technique. They relate to parts of the body as well as to the body as a whole moving through space. Gaining a precise sense of these directions begins with locating anatomical points of front, side, and back on the body.

Dancers move in space on three planes: frontal, sagittal, and transverse (see figure 5.19). The frontal plane is vertical and dissects the body front to back. The sagittal plane is also vertical but dissects the body into left and right halves. The transverse plane splits the body into upper and lower halves. Understanding these planes connects to understanding how movement, movement principles, and ballet aesthetics are related. To understand how the planes relate to your movement, you need to know your own body within these planes. Each dancer has unique physical attributes, so developing a sense of your body's positioning and direction is an individual task.

A directional sense of the body is a sense of the body as it moves forward, backward, or to either side in space. Developing this sense may seem simple, but it is in fact complex. Your body can move horizontally in any of these directions, but you must also be confident in moving down, rising, or jumping vertically or through the air. In addition, your body moves in these directions while also doing steps, which may move in a variety of directions, and possibly while using arm movements, which may go in other directions. Further complicating this equation is the fact that the head may face a variety of directions, too. Although all this complexity poses a challenge, it also adds to the interest and the fun of ballet.

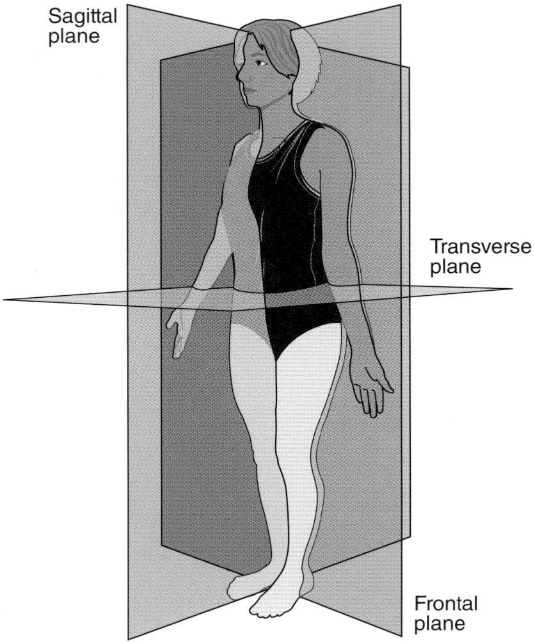

Figure 5.19 Planes of the body.

DIRECTIONS OF THE FEET

The working foot moves in various directions (figure 5.20). The basic directions include

* **devant** (to the front),
* **à la seconde** (to the second position), and
* **derrière** (to the back).

Exercises and steps use leg and foot movements or gestures that extend to the front, side, and back of the body or move in either angular or circular patterns. When performing barre exercises from first, third, or fifth positions, the body markers identified in the "Directions of the Feet" activity change. Practicing clear directions helps you acquire a directional acuity or clarity of movement.

TYPES OF BARRE COMBINATIONS

In many academic classes, you apply theories and practice applications to solve sets of problems. These problems become more complex as you learn more theories and concepts to apply. You encounter a similar process in ballet class.

In beginning ballet class, exercises and steps combine to become longer combinations. When you execute these combinations, you practice various movement sequences in all directions and for a number of repetitions. Executing combinations also presents inherent problems for you to solve, such as how, when, and where to move parts of the body to the music. Solving these movement problems is a

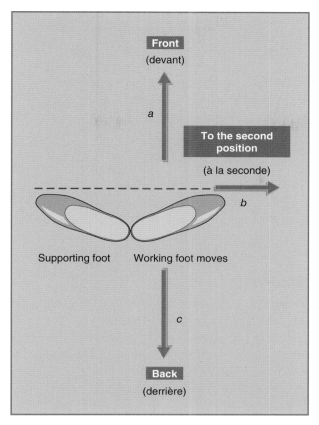

Figure 5.20 Directions of the feet.

ACTIVITY

Directions of the Feet

Find each of these directions:

Devant: Begin standing in first position and use the right leg as the working leg. Stretch the foot on the floor in front of you to a pointed position in line with your right ear. Later when you begin in fifth position, the line will shift to under your nose.

À la seconde: Begin standing in first position and use the right leg as the working leg. Stretch the foot on the floor toward the right under your right shoulder. The working great toe should point in a straight line with the great toe of the supporting foot.

Derrière: Begin standing in first position and use the right leg as the working leg. Stretch the foot on the floor behind you to a point in line with your right ear. Later when you begin in fifth position, the line shifts to the center back of your head.

Now, repeat the activity using the left foot as the working foot. Gaining a sense of direction for your feet and legs is vital to executing combinations. Together these directions combine to create patterns when you dance.

less daunting task when you know that combinations are based on patterns. All directional and patterns of barre exercises relate to the center line that divides the body into two symmetrical halves. Understanding directions and patterns helps you think on your feet and prepares you for complex combinations as you build your movement vocabulary.

While performing beginning combinations, you learn to apply movement principles such as when you anticipate changes in weight and direction. Continued practice performing combinations helps to increase your skill and expand your problem-solving abilities that lead you toward the goal of learning to execute barre combinations proficiently. Learning standard patterns at the barre is the first step toward this goal.

En Croix Pattern

Executing an exercise front, side, back, and side makes the **en croix** (in the shape of a cross) pattern (figure 5.21). The en croix pattern is the basis from which the number of repetitions of the exercise increases or decreases. The number of repetitions can extend to practicing a step four to eight times en croix, or decrease from four to two and later to one time en croix. Changing from four times en croix to two times or one time en croix takes mental preparation for these directional changes. This task can be challenging because of all the things you have to think about while executing the exercise. Performing an exercise en croix a number of times builds strength in the supporting leg and develops a spatial sense of front (devant), side (à la seconde), and back (derrière) directions, all in relation to body features.

Grasping the system of repetitions and directions takes time for your body and your mind to understand and use, especially since you have to think through the sequence of movements that make up each exercise.

Other Barre Patterns

You may encounter other patterns beyond the en croix pattern later in your beginning ballet course. For example, when facing the barre, alternating working legs enables the supporting leg to quickly assume weight, stance, and balance while the working leg executes the exercise.

Another pattern sometimes used later in the beginning course is front, back, and two repetitions to the side. As in en croix, steps in this pattern may be repeated four times, eight times, two times, or once.

Although most of the barre exercises are performed using these patterns, another type of pattern used at the barre is a half circle of the working leg on the ground. Generally, these circular patterns emanate from the

TECHNIQUE TIP ▶▶▶▶▶▶

Remembering the sequence of movements and visualizing the combination are vital to learning the combination. Saying the action words to yourself is another way to remember the combination. Repeating these words while you run the images of the movement sequence in your head strings together the movements.

hip so that the whole leg moves or the lower leg from the knee can describe a circular or angular pattern.

Barre exercises often combine two or more steps together. Usually the exercises complement one another in tempo, pattern, or design and extend the range of the first exercise. Or, they may be traditionally performed together, such as battement frappé and petit battement sur le cou-de-pied combinations.

Preparations and Endings at the Barre

Exercises at the barre and combinations in the center begin with a preparation—an introductory movement to music. They also include an ending. The preparation and ending have several functions:

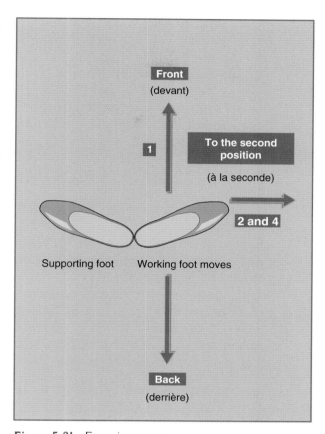

Figure 5.21 En croix pattern.

* To establish your presence as a performer
* To gain the attention of your audience
* To set the tempo and tone for executing the combination

Preparations should be executed with attention to poise and your presence as a dancer, showing your confidence to gain the attention of the audience to watch you perform the combination. Using preparations and endings, the dancer establishes a professional attitude, which is part of developing artistry at the beginning level of ballet.

At the barre, the preparation is a port de bras and it may include a preparatory movement of the working foot. Standing in the beginning position, either one or both arms execute the first port de bras. If you are facing the barre, then at the end of the first port de bras both hands rest on the barre shoulder-width apart. An alternative placement is to rest the hands on the barre with the wrists crossed.

If you use one hand on the barre, you may execute the first port de bras with either one or two arms. If you use one arm, then place the hand nearest the barre in front of the inside shoulder with the elbow down. If you use two arms, then when the arms reach second position, rest the hand nearest the barre on the barre in front of the inside shoulder, elbow down. The outside arm may remain in second position, return to preparatory position, or assume another position before the exercise begins.

At the end of an exercise, the working foot closes in the final foot position and the arms descend to preparatory position; you hold this position. Usually the arm and foot movements happen at the same time at the end of the music, signaling that the exercise is complete. You could think about it as the period to a movement sentence.

TYPES OF CENTER COMBINATIONS

In the center section of the beginning ballet class you explore a wide variety of slow and continuous, or adagio, and fast and lively, or allegro, combinations. Center combinations begin simply as practice of one step. Foot directions and the en croix pattern provide the design framework for center barre practice, which tests your balance and helps you gain strength and stability without the use of the barre. Adagio combinations are directional, repeating the same pose or movement that gradually extends for longer musical phrases.

After you become comfortable with allegro one-step combinations, two-step combinations are introduced to practice linking steps. By the end of the term, allegro combinations usually include three different steps.

Preparations and Endings in the Center

When preparing to execute a combination in the center, you face the beginning direction, assume the beginning foot and preparatory arm position, and listen for the musical introduction. During the introduction, you execute a preparation of a port de bras that may or may not be accompanied by a foot movement. At the end of the combination, you close in the ending foot position, your arms descend to preparatory position, and you hold this final position.

Dynamics of Center Combinations

Similar to the barre, in the center part of class, a traditional ballet preparation and ending frame a combination. If the purpose of the combination is to practice a specific step, then executing it on both sides of the body is the focus.

A goal in the beginning class is to execute beginning ballet vocabulary of exercises and steps with fundamental competency. This means knowing and executing steps and then in combinations of one or more steps. Memorizing the foot and leg actions of one exercise or step takes time. Compounding this type of memorization develops a strong connection between body and mind that is an integral part of learning and performing ballet technique. Generally a three-step combination has a pattern to it. Usually the first step is an introductory step, followed by two steps or one major step repeated, and an ending step. Although the combination has three steps, the repetition of the major step or two steps completes the standard four-measure musical phrase.

Alternating Combinations

As with barre exercises, all center combinations are performed starting on both sides. This alternating format helps you practice moving to both sides and balance the development of both sides of the body. First, you perform one side of the combination and you rest before executing the second side. Later you perform both sides of the combination or repeat these alternations a number of times to extend the length of the combination.

Center combinations can move side to side, in different directions, or across the floor, so you have to anticipate changes in direction while keeping your personal space and dancing with your group or the class. In beginning ballet, the major change of direction usually happens after the end of the combination when you begin the alternate side. Later these changes of direction can become part of a combination as steps move to one direction and then another.

SUMMARY

Basics of ballet technique cover the five positions of the feet, positions of the arms, and port de bras. Movement principles underlie moving from position to position in dancing combinations. The beginning ballet class includes some standard patterns for performing exercises at the barre and combinations in the center. As part of dancing in the center, practicing body directions and movement in relation to stage directions attunes you to performing in a variety of spaces. Likewise, beginning center combinations require replicating steps and learning to transfer the movement starting on the other foot.

To find supplementary materials for this chapter such as learning activities, e-journaling assignments, and web links, visit the web resource at www.HumanKinetics.com/BeginningBalletIE.

WEB RESOURCE

Chapter **6**

At the Barre

The barre is the first part of the ballet class, which lays the foundation for technique. At the barre, you learn, practice, and refine exercises and steps. Beginning the class at the barre gets you in tune with your body, your mind, and movement.

Barre has two meanings: It is a wooden rail that dancers uses to refine balance while performing exercises, and it is a series of exercises that warm up the body and develop skill for executing steps in the center. This chapter covers the series of exercises that comprise the pre-barre exercises, which prepare the dancer for the beginning barre and center with additional basic ballet exercises.

In the beginning ballet class, you perform barre exercises first facing the barre and later with one hand resting on the barre. When standing at the barre, you must follow certain protocols, including the following:

- Determine your personal space with respect to extension of legs and arms.
- Traditionally each exercise begins with the right foot.

◆ Before the music starts for each exercise, stand in position with your arms in preparatory position to demonstrate that you are physically and mentally ready to begin moving.

◆ To end each exercise, hold the final foot position with your arms in preparatory position to show completion of the movement.

Your teacher may present different or additional rules and protocols depending on the setting or the intent of the class. Chapter 2 covers general rules and protocols for ballet class.

STANDING AT THE BARRE

Choosing a place at the barre may be up to you, or the instructor may determine your position for you. Selecting a place at either end of the barre comes with a responsibility to be able to perform the exercise immediately following the teacher presenting the exercise, and leading other students on one side. Repeating the exercise on the other side, you must be able to transpose it using the other working leg. If you have a choice, decide whether you are ready for that challenge.

Facing the Barre

When you are facing the barre you have to establish a comfortable distance from the barre. Place your elbows at the sides of your body and place your hands on top of the barre, resting the fingers around the barre. Your forearms stretch forward with your hands placed on the barre in line with the shoulders, or they can cross near the wrists with your hands placed lightly around the barre (figure 6.1). You may have to move either forward or backward to find the right distance for you in relation to the barre.

One Hand on the Barre

To establish a comfortable distance when standing with one hand at the barre, place the hand in front of you and on the top of the barre, resting the fingers around the barre (figure 6.2). The elbow should remain bent, down, and near the side of your body and should not lift; lifting the elbow disturbs body alignment and balance. The position of your hand on the barre may adjust either forward or backward during an exercise. When the working leg extends back above 45 degrees, slide the hand on the barre forward during the counterbalance and slide it back when the you return to a vertically aligned position. After completing a barre exercise using one hand on the barre, you may bring the arm nearest the barre down to the preparatory position, turn toward the barre to change directions, and perform the second side.

> ### TECHNIQUE TIP ▸▸▸▸▸
>
> Traditionally dancers begin standing with the left hand on the barre, and the right foot, which is the outside foot, begins the exercise. Then, dancers turn to execute the exercise beginning with the left foot as the outside foot.

Figure 6.1 Facing the barre: *(a)* arms forward; *(b)* forearms crossed at the barre.

PRE-BARRE EXERCISES

Pre-barre exercises warm up body parts, increase flexibility and articulation, and help you acquire the right mindset and breathing for the barre exercises that follow. Specifically, pre-barre exercises warm up the legs, feet, hips, knees, and ankles. The pre-barre warm-up may be part of your class or you may choose to perform a personal pre-barre warm-up to prepare for the class. Later pre-barre exercises can be incorporated into barre or center barre exercises.

Foot Exercises

Foot exercises help you acquire basic foot skills that include pointing and flexing, presses, pedals, and flicks. All of these skills prepare you for pointing the foot, three-quarter rises (relevés), balances, and jumps. Practicing foot

Figure 6.2 One hand on the barre.

exercises develops articulation in the foot and ankle, which is critical for ballet technique. Foot exercises apply movement principles that increase balance on two legs and one, weight shifting, pull-up (lift), and alignment. These exercises are a prelude to foot movements at the barre, in center barre, and during center combinations.

Basic foot exercises are repeated eight times, four times, twice, or once on one foot before executing the same number of repetitions on the other foot. The challenge increases if the exercise transfers from one foot to the other with fewer repetitions because it requires quick thinking about each part of the exercise and simultaneous application of movement principles. Placing your hands or fingertips on the top of the barre or taking your hands off the barre during foot exercises increases the challenge for balance, which helps you later when you dance in the center.

Points and Flexes

Pointing the working foot on the floor or in the air is part of the ballet aesthetic. How you point the foot is important in developing your technique and line. The pointed foot begins with the ankle joint. The top of the foot stretches long while lifting the arch and the heel upward toward the leg. The foot becomes an extension of the lower leg. When a foot points, the toes stretch long as in the **pointe tendue** position on the floor where only the tips of the first, second, and third toes touch the floor. In the air, the toes extend long as part of the foot (figure 6.3). When the foot points and the toes stretch in the air as a result of brushing, rising, or jumping, this extension reverses through the toes, metatarsals, and heel into a demi-plié. The flexibility and articulation of the foot allow you to handle weight changes from two feet to one or from one foot to the other. When you pull up, these foot and leg movements with weight changes seem to be effortless. To prepare for these important uses of the pointed foot, practice this foot exercise at the barre.

Flexing the foot is the reverse of pointing the foot. **Foot flexion** begins at the ankle joint with the heel pushing forward. The flexion continues through the foot with the toes pulling back toward the working leg (figure 6.4).

Figure 6.3 Pointed foot *(a)* on the floor and *(b)* in the air.

Facing the barre and starting in first position, brush the right foot devant to a full pointed position. Begin the flexion with the heel pushing forward and articulating the movement throughout the entire foot and toes. Then reverse the movement to a fully pointed foot and toes.

Although the point and flex is explained devant, it is executed in à la seconde, derrière, and in an en croix pattern. Most often the point and flex combination repeats eight, four, or two times in each direction. You can perform this exercise both with the point first on the floor and later off the floor. During the exercise, the working and the supporting legs remain turned out.

Figure 6.4 Flexed foot.

▶ Foot Presses

The **foot press** stretches the foot from the full-foot position to the three-quarter relevé position with the toes and metatarsals resting on the floor. In first position, the heel releases and continues through the foot until the toes and metatarsals remain on the floor. The goal of the foot press is to lift the foot to where it is perpendicular to the floor while the metatarsals and all of the toes rest on the floor. On the return to the full-foot position, the heel resists as the foot returns to the floor. To cultivate power and strength, use the image of resisting against an outside force on the downward path. Likewise, visualize a direct path upward and downward along an imaginary line that bisects the foot triangle. This helps make kinesthetic connections to correct landings that center over the foot triangle.

▶ Foot Pedals

The **foot pedal** is an extension of the foot press with the entire foot releasing from the floor to a pointed position. The action begins with a quick release from the ankle through the foot. The tips of the toes on the pointed foot rest either on the floor or just above it.

The foot pedal is generated through the foot action of pushing the foot either to the point on the floor or pointing downward just off the floor. The knee bends as a result of the push action, and a line extends from the lower leg through the pointed foot. On the return action, the toes touch the floor first, followed by articulation through the metatarsals and foot to the full-foot position.

You can perform the sequence of the foot pedals all on one foot and then the other, in parallel first position, or in turned-out first or fifth position. Changing from foot to foot with the body lifted and supported during the foot pedals can be a challenge. To up the ante, rest only the fingertips on the barre; or, for the ultimate challenge, take your hands off the barre. It may be difficult at first, but practicing this skill helps you control your balance and your weight transfer while maintaining a quick, lifted torso with the abdominal muscles engaged in preparation for dancing in the center.

▶ Flicks and Presses

Another foot exercise combination is the **flick and press**. This exercise helps you develop the skill of flicking the foot quickly from a full-foot position to a point off the floor that begins at the ankle joint. The return press can be either a slow or fast articulation. Like other foot exercises, you can perform the flick and press on one foot several times, then repeat it using the other foot for the same number of repetitions. You can decrease the number of repetitions, which requires more attention to weight transfer. Practicing weight transfer after each flick and press while maintaining a quick, lifted torso with the abdominal muscles engaged prepares you for executing center steps.

▶ Relevé

After practicing foot presses, the next progression is **relevé**. In ballet shoes, use the three-quarter position, where the toes and metatarsals rest on the floor (figure 6.5). Begin by executing a demi-plié and quickly release the heels simultaneously in first, second, or third position to three-quarter relevé.

Balancing in three-quarter relevé, you can release your hands from the barre. The balance can last for 4 to 8 counts or longer. Before returning to the full-foot position, you can either return your hands to the barre or leave your hands off the barre.

Active-Foot Positions

In an active-foot position, the working leg is on or off the floor and positioned at different places on the supporting leg. These places can be at the front or back at the ankle, the middle of the lower leg, under the knee, or at the side of the knee. Chapter 5 presents a general overview of the types of active-foot positions. These active-foot positions begin from a classical foot position, most often fifth position. From a full-foot position, the working foot peels off the floor to a pointed position. Meanwhile, weight quickly shifts to the supporting leg, the abdominal muscles engage, and the torso pulls up as the body weight centers and aligns over the supporting leg.

SAFETY TIP ▶▶▶▶▶▶▶▶▶▶▶▶▶▶▶▶▶▶▶

Practicing pre-barre warm-up exercises before your class begins or as part of the class prepares your body to meet the continuing demands of barre exercises, prevents injuries, and prepares you for stretching exercises later in the class. You can create a warm-up that includes both general and specific exercises you have identified as beneficial to you personally and to avoid injuries.

Figure 6.5 Three-quarter relevé.

Figure 6.6 Pointe tendue.

Pointe tendue (stretched point): The foot points on the floor in various directions or as part of poses (figure 6.6).

B+ (attitude derrière pointe tendue à terre): Standing on one foot, the back leg bends at the knee with the foot pointed and the tip of the great toe touching the floor. In traditional B+ position, women keep their knees together and men have their knees slightly apart (figure 6.7). The B+ position is an alternative beginning position to fifth position for combinations in the center or across the floor.

Sur le cou-de-pied (on the neck of the foot): You can perform this position on the front or back of the supporting foot. In sur le cou-de-pied, the working foot is placed in various positions (figure 6.8), depending on the ballet method being followed.

Figure 6.7 B+ position.

In the Cecchetti method, the toes and metatarsals of the working foot rest on the floor either in front of or behind the ankle of the supporting foot (figure 6.8b). Beginning dancers often use this position in petit battement sur le cou-de-pied.

Figure 6.8 *(a)* Sur le cou-de-pied devant; *(b)* sur le cou-de-pied devant, practicing with the toes and metatarsals on the floor. This Cecchetti method alternative position is used to learn petit battement sur le cou-de-pied.

Later, the toes and metatarsals release from the floor to a pointed position either in front or behind the ankle.

In the Russian method, the working foot flexes at the ankle so that it is parallel to the floor with the toes pulled upward. The inside of the working heel rests on the top of the ankle bone of the supporting foot, directly in front or behind. This version of the position is often used in battement frappé and petit battement sur le cou-de-pied.

Coupé devant (cut front): The working leg bends at the knee. The foot points and the side of the little toe of the working foot touches the front of the supporting leg midway between the knee and the ankle (figure 6.9).

Coupé derrière (cut back): The working leg bends at the knee. The foot points and the inside of the heel touches the back of the supporting leg midway between the knee and ankle (figure 6.10).

Retiré devant (withdrawn front): The side of the little toe rests under the knee on the front of the supporting leg (figure 6.11).

Retiré derrière (withdrawn back): The inside of the heel of the working foot rests behind the knee of the supporting leg (figure 6.12).

▶ **Relevé (raised) in first position:** Standing in first position, the legs demi-plié and rise to three-quarter relevé, to where the toes and metatarsals rest on the floor. On the return, feet lower together into the full-foot position and the legs demi-plié.

▶ **Relevé (raised) in second position:** Standing in second position, the legs demi-plié and rise to three-quarter relevé; the toes and metatarsals rest on the floor.

Figure 6.9 Coupé devant.

Figure 6.10 Coupé derrière.

Figure 6.11 Retiré devant.

Figure 6.12 Retiré derrière.

On the return, the feet lower together to the full-foot position and the legs demi-plié.

Relevés are executed in all positions of the feet. Often beginning dancers practice four or eight relevés in a position and then finish with balancing en relevé (in raised position) with or without hands on the barre. If the relevés are done in more than one position, the working leg does a pointe tendue to change from one position to the next.

▶ **Sous-sus (under-over):** Starting in fifth position, the legs demi-plié and spring on to three-quarter relevé with both feet. Both legs and feet press against one another in the fifth position en relevé position. To descend, the torso lifts to allow both feet to simultaneously slide down into fifth position and the legs demi-plié.

BARRE EXERCISES

The barre exercises presented in this chapter follow the order in which they are performed in the traditional ballet barre. In the beginning ballet class, the barre exercises may not be taught in this order, but by the end of the term, the barre will contain most of the exercises in this chapter. Different methods of ballet execute the barre exercises in a similar but sometimes different order.

Each barre exercise includes its written pronunciation, definition, purpose, and description. In the web resource that accompanies this book, the ballet term is pronounced in the French language and a video clip presents the exercise. Also included is a self-check list for performing the exercise. Some basic barre exercises are followed by variations. Often these variations are practiced either as separate exercises or with the basic exercise for extended combinations.

Barre exercises begin in classical foot positions. In the beginning ballet class, you learn exercises starting in first position and then move to starting in either third position or fifth position (see chapter 5).

Before each exercise you stand in the beginning position and execute a preparation to music. In some cases the preparation is a port de bras, but for some exercises, foot movements accompany the port de bras as part of the preparation. In a beginning ballet class, the preparation may use four or two bars of music before the exercise begins.

▶ Demi-Plié [duh-MEE plee-AY]

Definition
Half bend of the knees

Purpose
- Warms up the hip, knee, and ankle joints
- Increases strength and flexibility of the lower leg
- Applies the principles of alignment, stance, turnout, and weight distribution

Description
To execute a demi-plié, stand in a classical position of the feet. Descend as far as the knees can bend with the entire foot remaining on the floor, then return to the starting position. Perform the demi-plié in first, second, third, fourth, then fifth position.

Maintaining turnout from the hips, bend the knees directly above the second and third toes of each foot. In second position, bend the legs half as much as for a grand plié.

▶ Grand Plié [grahn plee-AY]

Definition

Large bend of the knees

Purpose

* Stretches the muscles of the inner thigh in addition to those of the lower leg
* Applies the principles of alignment, turnout, weight distribution, squareness, and counterpull

Description

First, execute a demi-plié and then descend deeper to where the thighs are parallel to the floor. The heels release from the floor only as necessary on the descent and return as soon as possible on the ascent. Both knees bend and straighten simultaneously.

Performed in all foot positions, the grand plié is a continuous vertical movement, using the same number of measures for the descent and the ascent. The body weight is equally distributed over both legs. As you descend, the body counterpulls upward. On the ascent, the body remains lifted, appearing to float over the legs.

In second position, the space between the feet varies from one and 1/2 lengths of your foot to shoulder width. In this position you descend until the thighs are parallel to the floor, but the full foot remains on the floor throughout the grand plié.

▶ Battement Tendu [bat-MAHN than-DEW]

Definition

Stretched beating

Purpose

* Increases flexibility of the ankle
* Develops full extension and proper alignment of the foot with the leg
* Applies principles of alignment, stance, turnout, weight distribution, weight transfer, and squareness

Description

Start in first position at the beginning and later start in third or fifth position. From a full-foot position, brush the working foot along the floor extending through the arch, then the metatarsals, to a fully pointed position. In the pointed position, the tips of the first three toes rest on the floor and the heel is lifted high and forward. On the return path the foot flexes first through the toes, then the metatarsals, the arch, and finally to the full-foot position as it slides back to the closing. Practice battement tendu devant, à la seconde, and then derrière. For the battement tendu à la seconde, slide the working foot to a point that is in line with the great toe of the supporting foot (Cecchetti method) or in line with the supporting heel (Russian method).

▶ Battement Tendu With Demi-Plié
[bat-MAHN than-DEW with duh-MEE plee-AY]

Definition
Stretched beating with half bend

Purpose
* Connects two exercises seamlessly
* Coordinates movements of the supporting leg with the working leg (the working leg does the out and in movement, while the supporting leg does the down and up movement)

Description
The battement tendu with demi-plié is two exercises combined. On the return path of the battement tendu, the working and supporting legs execute a demi-plié. Both legs reach the depth of the demi-plié when the working foot reaches the closed position. From the demi-plié, the next battement tendu begins with each leg simultaneously straightening on the extension section ending when the working foot is fully pointed.

▶ Battement Tendu Relevé
[bat-MAHN than-DEW ruhl-VAY]

Definition
Stretched and raised beating

Purpose
* Develops skills in transferring weight from two feet to one foot and back to two feet
* Challenges balance

Description
The battement tendu relevé begins with the extension of the working leg to a point. Shift the weight from the supporting leg to equally on both legs. The working foot accepts the weight through the toes to the full-foot position. To bring the weight back to the supporting leg, it pulls up to accept the weight as the working foot points and brushes back to the beginning position. You can perform battement tendu relevé without or with a demi-plié when the weight shifts to both legs in the full-foot position. After the working foot returns to the pointed position, it brushes back to the beginning position in demi-plié.

Dancers executing battement dégagé or jeté at the barre.

▶ Battement Dégagé or Jeté
[bat-MAHN day-ga-ZHAY or zhuh-TAY]

Definition

Beating disengaged (dégagé) from (Cecchetti method) or thrown (jeté) from (Russian method) the floor

Purpose

* Facilitates sharp, quick, small movements of the entire working leg and foot in all directions
* Develops complete foot articulation and extension of the ankle
* Applies principles of alignment, turnout, stance, weight distribution, and transfer of weight

Description

From a full-foot position, brush the working foot strongly through the battement tendu and extend the pointed foot off the floor. The battement extends approximately 2 to 3 inches (5-7 cm), or about 20 degrees off the floor. On the return, move the working foot through the pointed position to the floor and brush back to the full-foot position.

▶ Petit Battement Piqué [puh-TEE bat-MAHN pee-KAY] or Battement Tendu Jeté Pointe [bat-MAHN than-DEW zhuh-TAY pwen-TAY]

Definition

Stretched beating, thrown and pointed

Purpose

- Uses the turned-out leg and pointed foot as a unit
- Develops directional acuity

Description

Brush the working foot off the floor in a battement dégagé. With the knee stretched and the foot pointed, the great toe lightly touches or taps (piqués) the floor and rebounds to battement dégagé. You may execute more than one piqué in a direction before closing or moving to the next direction.

▶ Battement Dégagé en Cloche [bat-MAHN day-ga-ZHAY ahn klawsh]

Definition

Disengaged beating while swinging like a clapper in a bell

Purpose

- Develops freedom of the working leg, moving from the hip joint both front and back
- Challenges the control of the back and hips while retaining balance and stability of the standing leg
- Requires the body to remain square, pulled up, and quiet during the swinging movements

Description

Brush the working foot from a full-foot position to a battement dégagé. Then, sweep the working foot through first position to the opposite direction: devant (front) or derrière (back). This exercise is often performed in a series and may end in a closed or open position.

Rond de Jambe à Terre [rawn duh zhahmb ah tehr]

Definition

Circular movement of the leg described by the pointed foot on the floor (the circular movement describes a half circle in two directions)

Purpose

- Develops the rotary movement of the entire working leg and foot in a turned-out position in both directions

- Isolates movement of the working leg and foot while the pelvis remains stationary
- Applies principles of alignment, turnout, and weight distribution

Description

The rond de jambe à terre preparation changes as the beginning ballet class progresses. For a simple preparation, begin in either first or fifth position and execute a battement tendu à la seconde, then close in first position. As you gain experience, execute a battement tendu devant with the supporting leg in demi-plié. As the working leg executes a demi-rond de jambe to à la seconde, the supporting leg straightens and then the leg and pointed foot move to pointe tendue derrière as preparation for a series of ronds de jambe. If you begin the rond de jambe à terre dedans as a separate exercise, the preparation begins by brushing the working foot to pointe tendue derrière and executing a demi-rond de jambe en dedans to à la seconde, the supporting leg straightens, and then the leg and pointed foot move to pointe tendue devant as preparation for a series of ronds de jambe en dedans.

▶ Rond de Jambe à Terre en Dehors
[rawn duh zhahmb ah tehr ahn duh-AWR]

Definition

Circular movement of the leg, on the floor, outward and away from the supporting leg

Description

Brush the working foot from pointe tendue either à la seconde or derrière to full-foot position in first position to a pointe tendue devant (front). The working leg describes a half circle with the great toe in contact with the floor through à la seconde and derrière, or clockwise. Usually you execute eight ronds de jambe à terre en dehors before reversing the direction of the exercise.

▶ Rond de Jambe à Terre en Dedans
[rawn duh zhahmb ah tehr ahn duh-DAHN]

Definition

Circular movement of the leg, on the floor, inward toward the supporting leg

Description

The rond de jambe à terre en dedans travels in the reverse direction to en dehors. The working foot describes a half circle with the great toe in contact with the floor beginning in pointe tendue à la seconde or devant brushing through full-foot first position to derrière, à la seconde, and devant, or counterclockwise. Usually you execute eight ronds de jambe à terre en dedans.

While the working leg is moving, the supporting leg is turned out and pulled up with the weight centered over the foot triangle. The body is square and the hips quiet to allow the working leg to rotate in the hip joint.

Port de Corps [pawr duh kawr]

Definition

Translated, the term means carriage of the body. As part of the ballet barre the term refers to bending the torso forward, side, or back. Cambré [kauhm-BRAY], a similar term, refers to bending to the side or the back.

Purpose

- Develops flexibility in the torso
- Establishes a stable base of legs and hips as part of stance
- Practices coordination of arms and head as the body moves
- Applies principles of squareness, lift, alignment, turnout, and balance on two feet

Description

Execute port de corps front, back, or to the side (can be done in all five full-foot positions). Begin in a vertically aligned position. Inhale and stretch the body upward before bending. During the bend, exhale. On the return, inhale as you stretch the torso in a larger arc back to the vertically aligned position. The stretch is continuous and smooth throughout. Accompany the port de corps with port de bras. The port de corps directions may be performed together as an individual exercise or in combination with other barre exercises, such as following rond de jambe à terre.

Dancers demi-plié at the end of a battement tendu with demi-plié exercise.

▶ Port de Corps Devant [pawr duh kawr duh-VAHN]

Definition

Carriage of the body to the front

Description

When doing the port de corps devant, you have a choice of two paths. You can roll down and up, or you can bend and return to vertical alignment with a flat back.

- *Path 1: Rolling down and rolling up.* Stretch the body upward in an aligned position. Bend your head forward, and curve your spine down to the hips. As your back rounds, engage the abdominals and keep the pelvis centered over the legs. At the end of the roll-down, the torso stretches long toward the floor. On the return path, the back uncurls one vertebra at a time to the vertically aligned position; the head is the last to return. Simultaneously stretch the legs upward form the floor.

- *Path 2: Flat back, or hinge and reverse hinge.* Stretch the body upward in an aligned position and tilt the torso forward at the hips to a 90-degree angle, or hinge position. The back continues to stretch downward toward the floor. The legs remain perpendicular, with the body weight equally shared over both foot triangles. Lead with the head on the return path with the neck and back stretching outward and upward through the flat-back position to a vertically aligned position. Engage the abdominals as the back, neck, and head stretch upward in a wider arc than the downward path. Simultaneously stretch the legs upward from the floor.

As a beginner, keep your head in a centered position. This position helps support squareness in the shoulders and hips. Later, you may turn the head toward the outside shoulder.

▶ Port de Corps Derrière [pawr duh kawr dehr-YEHR]

Definition

Carriage of the body to the back

Description

In an aligned position, stretch upward and then begin stretching backward with the head centered and the neck lengthened. Continue the bend through the upper back to the waist (Cecchetti method). Keep the abdominals engaged and the pelvis centered and quiet. Some styles of ballet allow the bend to continue to the hips (Russian method).

On the return path, the spine leads the unfolding from its base, articulating and stretching upward through the back, neck, and head until you reach vertical alignment. The head remains in a centered position. As you gain experience, you may turn the head toward the outside shoulder.

▶ Port de Corps à la Seconde
[pawr duh kawr ah lah suh-KOHND]

Definition

Carriage of the body to the side

Description

Begin in the vertically aligned body position. Stretch the torso upward and then bend the head, neck, and torso to the side as a unit. On the return to alignment, continue to stretch the body through a wider arc. The legs share the weight during the port de corps. Shoulders and hips are square at the beginning and end of the exercise.

▶ Battement Frappé [bat-MAHN fra-PAY]

Definition

Beating of the foot by striking the floor

Purpose

- Develops isolated movement in the lower leg and foot
- Builds flexibility in the ankle joint and develops foot articulation
- Applies principles of balance, pull-up, squareness, turnout, and alignment

Description

Position the working foot in either in the Cecchetti or the Russian versions of sur le cou-de-pied at the ankle. In the Cecchetti version, the toes and metatarsals rest on the floor, brushing quickly to extend the lower leg and the foot to a pointed position barely off the floor. In the Russian version, the heel of the working foot rests on the ankle of the supporting leg. The working foot flexes at the ankle with the toes and metatarsals flexed. From this position, extend the ankle so that the toes and metatarsals strike the floor near the ankle and quickly brush so that the lower leg straightens and the foot points off the floor.

Hold the stretched leg and foot position for a moment before snapping back to the sur le cou-de-pied position. Throughout the extension and return, keep the upper leg unmoving and turned out. Perform battement frappé in all directions. In à la seconde, the working foot rests either in front or behind the supporting ankle. To perform frappé derrière, rest the inside of the working ankle behind the supporting ankle.

▶ Petit Battement sur le Cou-de-Pied
[puh-TEE bat-MAHN sewr luh koo-duh-PYAY]

Definition

Small beating at the neck of the foot

Purpose

- Develops quick foot and lower leg gestures as the basis for allegro steps in the center

- Requires isolated movement of the lower working leg while the upper working leg remains stable and turned out
- Applies principles of turnout, balance on one leg, pull-up, and squareness

Description

The petit battement is a series of quick movements of the lower leg and foot describing a V-shaped pattern with the apex à la seconde, starting from the front or back sur le cou-de-pied. Keep the upper working leg well turned out and quiet. Center your body weight over the stretched supporting leg.

In the Russian method, the pointed working foot may be positioned at the ankle in the sur le cou-de-pied position, and it describes the V-shaped pattern in the air. In the Cecchetti method, the toes and metatarsals of the working foot rest on the floor in the sur le cou-de-pied position, and they describe the V-shaped pattern by gliding over the floor. As you gain experience, the foot position becomes pointed at the ankle with the V-shaped pattern described in the air.

▶ Battement Développé [bat-MAHN dayv-law-PAY]

Definition

Unfolding of the leg

Purpose

- Develops strength in the back and the supporting leg while the working leg extends in various directions
- Increases control of the working leg as it extends to positions up to 45 degrees
- Initiates an important component of adagio at the barre and especially for the center
- Applies the principles of balance on one leg, pull-up, counterbalance, squareness, turnout, alignment, and weight distribution

Description

Beginning in fifth position, release the working leg from the floor through the sur le cou-de-pied devant or derrière on the supporting leg in a straight line to either low (coupé) or standard retiré position (see figures 6.11 and 6.12). From this position extend the working leg devant, à la seconde, or derrière. In devant or à la seconde, the working heel leads the leg as it unfolds continuously to full extension to the same height as the thigh in the coupé or retiré. In derrière, the toes direct the extension of the lower leg to coupé or retiré height. Then, stretch the working leg and hold it at maximum extension before descending to a point on the floor and brushing back into fifth position. During the battement développé, lengthen the spine to keep the body in alignment over the supporting leg. In the battement développé derrière, when the working leg unfolds from retiré, you may move the back from an aligned position into counterbalance. As the working leg descends and closes in fifth position, return the back to its vertically aligned position.

▶ Grand Battement [grahn bat-MAHN]

Definition

Large beating or kicking action of the leg into the air

Purpose

- Develops flexibility and strength of the working leg muscles
- Promotes flexibility of the hip socket
- Applies principles of alignment, turnout, weight distribution, and transfer of weight

Description

Starting in first and later fifth position, brush the working leg through a battement tendu, dégagé, or jeté and continue to extend to approximately 45 and later 90 degrees in the air. This brushing action throws the leg into the air with a momentary pause at the height of the extension before a slower descent to or through the battement tendu and closing in the starting position. For the grand battement devant or à la seconde, the body remains vertically aligned and balanced on the supporting foot, the abdominals are engaged, and the torso is lifted off a pulled-up supporting leg. Executing the grand battement derrière, when the leg brushes off the floor, stretch the back upward and forward into a counterbalanced position and return to a vertically aligned position as the working foot brushes into the starting position. If a number of grand battements derrière is part of the exercise, the return to the aligned position occurs on the last battement.

During the term, beginning barre exercises are often combined with similar types of exercises to add complexity and duration. This progression further challenges you to develop strong technique and smooth transitions when going from one movement to another.

SUMMARY

The beginning ballet barre provides the basic exercises that support beginning center work and future ballet studies. Clearly understanding each exercise, its components, technical requirements, rhythm, and movement qualities establishes a strong basis from which to build ballet center steps and combinations.

To find supplementary materials for this chapter such as learning activities, e-journaling assignments, and web links, visit the web resource at www.HumanKinetics.com/BeginningBallet1E.

Chapter 7

In the Center

After barre work is completed, the ballet class moves to the middle of the studio. In the center section of the ballet class, dancers practice exercises from the barre and learn steps and combinations performed either slowly or quickly. In the center is where you learn to dance. The center has a structure and order of practice that may vary depending on the teacher or the method used.

Several categories of steps constitute the center part of class. In the beginning ballet class, these categories may not be taught in the standard sequence of a typical ballet class until a sufficient movement vocabulary allows these categories to emerge. The basic center structure will become apparent before the end of the term. This chapter presents the exercises and steps by category. Center barre replicates one or more exercises from the barre. Adagio combinations mesh exercises, poses, and steps with directional changes. Petit allegro steps and combinations use the range of footwork learned through the barre as part of steps that require quick thinking and moving. Grand allegro steps, poses, and combinations include steps that propel you off the ground and into the air before softly landing to ascend again.

RULES AND PROTOCOLS

For the center, the class moves quickly and quietly to fill the studio space. Ensure you have sufficient personal space and face the front of the studio. During the center part of class there are specific rules and protocols, including the following:

- *Know your stage directions.* Understanding and applying stage directions gives you a spatial awareness of the studio as a performance area or as preparation for performance on stage. The stage directions are from the perspective of the dancer (see figure 4.2).

- *Maintain personal space.* Since you and all the members of the class are either moving together in the studio or in small groups, you have to be aware of your personal space in relation to other people. Gaining spatial awareness is important for personal safety.

- *Begin on the right side.* Stand with the right foot forward and in position to execute the combination. The second time you perform the combination, be ready to begin with the left foot.

- *Change lines and groups efficiently.* For center combinations, changing lines efficiently saves time during class. See chapter 3 for more information.

- *Enter and exit the middle of the studio for group combinations.* To perform group combinations, you can come from one or both sides or the back of the studio. After the combination, you can exit to either side of the studio. Your teacher may designate the directions for entering or exiting. Knowing where the entrance and exits are makes for efficient transitions between groups in center combinations. Your teacher or the accompanist provides transitional music to allow groups to move in and out of the dancing space.

- *Move across the floor.* When you move across the floor either by yourself, in a line, or with a group, you must be safe and courteous. Performing as an individual, the goal is to move across the floor either in one or two repetitions of the combination. As part of a line or group, you dance together as you cross the floor. You must keep moving through the space; if another group follows and you haven't moved, people could collide. Each person participating in the combination has a responsibility to move across the floor efficiently to allow the next group the time and space to complete their combination. To learn about general rules and protocols for the ballet class, see chapter 2.

CENTER BARRE

Center barre, sometimes called center practice, consists of one or more exercises learned at the barre and practiced in the center. Practicing barre exercises in the center presents a challenge. In addition to performing the exercise, you work on maintaining alignment and turnout, transferring weight, and developing balance. Center barre exercises test how well you can execute the exercises without using the barre for support. The goal is to decrease your dependence on the barre so that you can successfully perform in the center.

Generally center barre exercises repeat in a series of eight in one direction, followed by eight in the other direction. Later the series can decrease to four and then to two steps or one step repeated several times. Two examples of center barre exercises practiced in the center are battement tendu and passé.

▶ Battement Tendu en Promenade [bat-MAHN than-DEW ahn prohm-NAHD]

Begin in first position and later in third or fifth position. This is a series of battements tendus à la seconde executed with alternating feet, closing in the starting position. The *en promenade* in the ballet term refers to walking either **en arrière** (backward) or **en avant** (forward).

▶ Battement Tendu en Croix [bat-MAHN than-DEW ahn kwah]

Battement tendu en croix is performed at the barre (see chapter 6) and is often part of center barre. You can do this exercise in first, third, or fifth position. You may do the exercise on one side followed by the other. To transfer to the other side using third or fifth position, the first en croix pattern ends with the working foot closing in fifth position behind so that you can be begin the pattern with the other foot.

▶ Passé [pa-SAY] en Promenade [ahn prohm-NAHD] en Arrière [ahn a-RYEHR] or en Avant [ahn a-VAHN]

The passé step learned at the barre is often performed as a series moving en arrière (backward) and then en avant (forward). Similar to the battement tendu en promenade, the passé step helps increase transfer of weight and balance while moving in these directions.

These center barre exercises help you to acquire the necessary balance, control of your body, and command of these steps and movement principles that contribute to learning more steps and gaining competency in center work. As the term progresses, you can practice the longer and more difficult barre exercises in the center.

PORT DE BRAS

Port de bras [pawr duh brah] translates as *carriage of the arms*. In the center, port de bras focuses on learning arm movements in various positions, sequences, and directions. As a singular exercise in the center, the practice of port de bras increases coordination of the arms in conjunction with small torso movements and breath to gain flowing, articulate arm movements that are later incorporated into combinations.

To create positions of the arms in classical ballet, stretch the entire arm and slightly flex the elbows and wrists to create a long, curved line through the arm and hand. Hold the arms in front of the body with the elbows out to the sides. Curve the hands with the palms facing the body on an angle in most classical arm positions. For a refresher on the classical arm positions, refer to chapter 5.

Classical Port de Bras

Port de bras is practiced as an individual exercise as well as part of the preparation for barre exercises or center combinations.

▶ First Port de Bras

Begin with the arms in preparatory position, or fifth position en bas. Raise both arms to first position, then open to second position. Rotate both arms as you lift the elbows slightly before floating downward and returning to your beginning position.

▶ Second Port de Bras

Begin with the arms in preparatory position, or fifth position en bas. Raise both arms to fifth position en haut. Open and rotate both arms as you move to second position. Then lift the elbows slightly before floating downward and returning to your beginning position.

ADAGIO

Adagio [a-DAZH-yoh] combinations encompass slow, sustained movements and poses. In these combinations, the dancer strives to perform positions, poses, and steps with an effortless, smooth quality. Some adagio steps are performed **à terre** (with the working foot on the floor); other steps are performed **en l'air** (with the working leg in the air). Beginning adagio combinations present a challenge to stretch the body line through the arms and legs or hold a leg in a position en l'air to create beautiful pictures, which requires strength and balance.

Adagio includes practicing classical positions and poses, which present you in frontal, crossed, or open directions. As a beginning dancer, learning these classical positions prepares you for integrating the positions and directions into combinations.

▶ Classical Positions of the Body

The **classical positions of the body** include eight basic positions, which you can perform as a combination or incorporate with other steps into combinations. When you study these positions, you learn body line, shading, and contrast. Moving from one position to the next in a series requires following several protocols.

- ◆ Open the working foot with the arms to create the position.
- ◆ Execute directional changes for the next position during the closing of the working leg into fifth position.
- ◆ After each body position, move the arms in an outward path and end in preparatory position, or fifth position en bas.

When performed in a sequence, the classical positions of the body become a combination, where you move smoothly from one position to the next. Practicing the battement tendu en croix combination establishes your acuity of basic front, side, and back as directions before integrating the combination with the more complex positions of the body and their directions. The body facing, arms, and head create each body position. Keep dancer stage directions in mind in relation to performing each classical position.

The classical positions in the next section use the sequence from the Cecchetti method. The Russian method uses a different sequence of positions and different arm placement for some of the positions. The following descriptions list stage directions for both the Russian method and the Cecchetti method. All of the positions are presented beginning from fifth position, right foot front, facing downstage corner 2 (Cecchetti) or 8 (Russian). Movement principles applied include squareness, pull-up, turnout, weight distribution, transfer of weight, and alignment.

Croisé Devant [kwah-ZAY duh-VAHN] (Crossed in the Front)

The body faces a downstage corner. Execute a battement tendu devant and extend the downstage, working leg and foot to a downstage corner. Extend the upstage arm overhead and the other in second position. The head turns with eyes focusing on the audience (figure 7.1).

À la Quatrième Devant [ah lah ka-tree-EM duh-VAHN] (to Fourth Position Front)

Facing downstage center or the audience, extend the working leg and pointed foot to the audience (direction 5 or 1). Extend the arms in second position. Your head faces the audience (figure 7.2).

Écarté Devant [ay-kar-TAY duh-VAHN] (Separated, Thrown Wide Apart in Front)

The body faces a downstage corner. Extend the working leg and pointed foot to the other downstage corner. The downstage arm is in fifth position en haut; the other arm is in second position. Lift your head up, so that your eyes focus on the palm of the hand en haut. This is the devant version of écarté (figure 7.3).

Figure 7.1 Croisé devant.

Effacé Devant [eh-fa-SAY duh-VAHN] (Shaded)

The body faces a downstage corner. Extend the working leg and pointed foot in front of the body. The downstage arm is in fifth position en haut; the upstage arm is in second position. Turn and lift your head upward to look toward the audience. Turn and tilt the upper torso and shoulders backward, opening toward the audience. This is the devant version of this body position (figure 7.4).

Figure 7.2 À la quatrième devant.

Figure 7.3 Écarté devant.

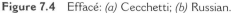

Figure 7.4 Effacé: *(a)* Cecchetti; *(b)* Russian.

À la Seconde [ah lah suh-KOHND] (to Second Position)

The body faces the audience, or downstage center. Extend the working leg and pointed foot à la seconde. Extend the arms in second position. Your head faces the audience (figure 7.5).

Épaulé [ay-poh-LAY] (Shouldered)

The body faces a downstage corner. Extend the working leg behind with the foot pointed to the opposite upstage corner. Extend the downstage arm forward at eye level; the upstage arm extends behind. Twist the upper torso to allow the arms to create a complete diagonal line. Lift the head and tilt it to the right. Focus the eyes on the fingertips of the forward hand (figure 7.6).

Figure 7.5 À la seconde.

À la Quatrième Derrière [ah lah ka-tree-EM dehr-YEHR] (to Fourth Position Back)

The body faces the audience. Extend the working leg and pointed foot à la quatrième derrière. Extend the arms in second position. Your head faces the audience (figure 7.7).

Croisé Derrière [kwah-ZAY dehr-YEHR] (Crossed in the Back)

The body faces a downstage corner. Extend the downstage, working leg and pointed foot back to the opposite upstage corner. Extend one arm to fifth position en haut and the other arm to second position.

Figure 7.6 Épaulé: *(a)* Cecchetti; *(b)* Russian.

Figure 7.7 À la quatrième derrière.

Turn the head and look under the right arm at the audience. Turn the body slightly and tilt on a diagonal from the shoulders through the working leg and foot (Cecchetti; figure 7.8*a*). In the Russian version, use the opposite arms. The head turns to look toward the audience over the downstage arm in second position (figure 7.8*b*).

Practice these positions as a sequence using battement tendu first on one side, then transferring the positions to the other side. Performing this sequence of classical body positions represents a significant accomplishment for you as a beginning ballet dancer.

Classical Poses and Steps

Ballet has two basic classical poses: the arabesque and the attitude. As a beginning dancer you learn arabesque and you may also study attitude.

Arabesque [a-ra-BESK]

The **arabesque** pose is a versatile pose with a number of variations in classical ballet. The term *arabesque* comes from a form of Moorish ornament. When in arabesque, you balance on one leg and extend the working leg behind at approximately 45 degrees; as you gain experience, the leg gets higher. Your stretched torso may use counter-

Figure 7.8 Croisé derrière: *(a)* Cecchetti; *(b)* Russian.

balance. The arms extend in various positions. In arabesque, the palms face downward. Arabesques are numbered and vary slightly depending on the method used.

The Cecchetti method has five arabesques. The first, second, and third arabesques are described as they are most used in beginning ballet technique The fourth and fifth arabesques are variations that may be included in the beginning ballet vocabulary. The Russian school uses four arabesques. Both styles are presented here.

▶ Cecchetti Method

♦ **First arabesque:** Your body is in profile to the audience. The supporting leg is the upstage leg, which is straight and turned out. As a beginner, your leg is generally no higher than 45 degrees. The forward arm is on the same side of the body as the supporting leg. The downstage arm opens to the side. In the Cecchetti method, you strive for square shoulders and hips. The upstage arm extends forward at eye level and your eyes focus beyond the fingertips. The downstage arm opens slightly behind second position so that both arms together create a diagonal line. Your eyes focus straight ahead (figure 7.9).

♦ **Second arabesque:** Your body is in profile to the audience. The upstage supporting leg is straight and turned out. The body line is square, yet open to the audience. The forward arm is on the same side of the body as the leg that extends behind. The other arm extends behind second position. The two arms create a complete diagonal line. Your eyes focus over the fingertips of your forward hand. Your head tilts toward the audience (figure 7.10).

♦ **Third arabesque:** Your body is in profile to the audience. The supporting leg is straight and turned out. Your body line strives for square shoulders and hips. Both arms are forward. The upper arm is away from the audience and

Figure 7.9 First arabesque, Cecchetti method.

Figure 7.10 Second arabesque, Cecchetti method.

Figure 7.11 Third arabesque, Cecchetti method.

extends level to the top of the forehead. The lower arm is nearest the audience and at shoulder height. Your eyes focus straight ahead as if you are looking through a window created by your arms (figure 7.11).

You can practice these three arabesques individually or together as an adagio combination. The adagio combination builds strength and challenges balance on the supporting leg while you change the arms from one arabesque pose to the next.

In the Cecchetti method, the fourth and fifth arabesques are variations of the first three. In **fourth arabesque** your body most often faces a down-stage corner (figure 7.12). The downstage leg is the supporting leg, similar to second arabesque, but in a demi-plié. The arms are the same as for first arabesque. Your head tilts toward the upstage arm and eyes focus to the downstage corner. In **fifth arabesque** your body faces a downstage stage corner; the supporting leg is the downstage leg in a demi-plié (figure 7.13). The arms are the same as for third arabesque. Your eyes focus toward the downstage corner.

▶ Russian Method

+ **First arabesque:** In first arabesque, the torso and downstage shoulder open from the bottom of the sternum. The forward arm is at shoulder height. The down-stage arm is in second position or slightly behind (figure 7.14).

+ **Second arabesque:** Similar to Russian first arabesque, your body is in profile with the supporting leg upstage from the audience. The downstage arm stretches forward while the upstage arm extends behind the body. The head turns to the audience (figure 7.15).

Figure 7.12 Fourth arabesque, Cecchetti method.

Figure 7.13 Fifth arabesque, Cecchetti method.

Figure 7.14 First arabesque, Russian method.

Figure 7.15 Second arabesque, Russian method.

+ **Third arabesque**: Your body faces a downstage corner. The downstage leg is straight and turned out. The upstage leg stretches behind in croisé derrière. The upstage arm extends forward, while the other arm opens in second position. Your face looks toward the forward hand (figure 7.16).

Figure 7.16 Third arabesque, Russian method.

Figure 7.17 Fourth arabesque, Russian method.

• **Fourth arabesque:** The legs are the same position as for third arabesque. The torso turns upstage; the downstage arm stretches forward and the upstage arm extends behind. The arms create a continuous line through the body. Your head looks toward the audience and tilts toward the downstage shoulder (figure 7.17).

Usually, you first learn arabesque facing the barre so that you can understand the relationships between the body, legs, arms, and head before practicing it in the center.

Arabesque Variations

Beginning-level variations of the arabesque pose include arabesque à terre and arabesque en fondu. **Arabesque à terre** is literally arabesque with the working foot resting on the floor (figure 7.18). **Arabesque en fondu** means arabesque melted. In this variation of the arabesque pose, the supporting leg is in fondu, or a demi-plié on one leg (figure 7.19).

▶ Battement Développé [bat-MAHN dayv-law-PAY]

You learn battement développé as a barre exercise before trying it as an adagio step in the center. You may execute one more battement développé in an adagio or perform a series of them en croix as part of an adagio. The battement développé is usually at a 45-degree angle or lower until you gain strength and flexibility. Before you lift the leg higher, be sure that you have control of alignment, turnout, and

Figure 7.18   Arabesque à terre.

Figure 7.19   Arabesque en fondu.

pull-up (lift) and you are able to balance on one foot while extending the leg in various directions at above 45 degrees.

INTRODUCTORY AND TRANSITIONAL STEPS

Combinations include introductory and transitional steps. These steps provide an introduction to a combination or a connection or preparation for the next step in the combination. Some of these steps help you change direction or transfer weight to the other foot.

▶ Ballet Walks

In ballet, you walk with the foot in a turned-out position. Starting in pointe tendue devant, the ballet walk begins with the toes. Transfer your weight from the toes, through the ball of the foot, and onto the full foot. When you execute a ballet walk, move smoothly with grace and poise.

▶ Pas de Bourrée [pah duh boo-RAY] (Stuffed Steps)

The pas de bourrée has the same name as a historical dance performed in the baroque period. It is three quick steps on alternating feet performed on three-quarter relevé. The basic step has variations in direction, such as dessous (under) or dessus (over).

Starting in third or fifth position, the back (left) leg does coupé derrière as you demi-plié the front (right) leg. Step en relevé behind with the right leg, step to first position with the right leg, and close with the left leg front in fifth position, demi-plié. You are now in position to repeat the step beginning with the right leg.

▶ Chassé à la Seconde [sha-SAY ah lah suh-KOHND] (Chasing Step to Second)

Starting in fifth position, demi-plié and transfer your weight to the back leg. Slide the front leg out to second position in demi-plié; the body lifts by the back leg pushing into the air. Extend both legs with feet fully pointed and meeting in fifth position in the air. The jump ends in demi-plié in the starting full-foot position. The chasing part of the step comes from the quick push from the back leg for the air moment.

▶ Chassé Devant [sha-SAY duh-VAHN] (Chasing Step Front)

Start in third or fifth position and demi-plié. Slide the front foot out into a short fourth position devant; the back leg pushes the body into the air. The legs meet in third or fifth position in the air before landing in demi-plié in third or fifth position. The chasing part of the step comes from the quick push from the back leg for the air moment.

▶ Glissade [glee-SAHD] (Gliding Step)

Start in demi-plié in third or fifth position. With the working leg, dégagé à la seconde. As you push off with the supporting leg, the body moves to the side. In the air moment, both legs and feet extend just above the floor. The first foot lands and the second foot quickly brushes into demi-plié in third or fifth position. You can perform glissade with the feet changing or not changing. During the glissade, the body pulls up to allow the legs and feet to execute the gliding movements.

▶ Balancé [ba-lahn-SAY] (Rocking Step)

The balancé can begin in either third or fifth position. The back leg demi-pliés while the front leg brushes to a dégagé à la seconde before stepping out onto it. The supporting foot touches in three-quarter relevé behind the front foot, which extends in a fully pointed position barely off the ground before the weight transfers to it. You can perform the balancé slowly as part of adagio or briskly as part of allegro, both side to side and front and back.

▶ Pas de Basque [pah duh bask] (Step of the Basque)

In the Russian version of this step, you begin facing a downstage corner and end the step facing the other downstage corner. Starting in demi-plié in fifth position, transfer the weight to the back leg. Brush the front foot à la seconde, and transfer the weight to it, pointing the other foot à terre. Slide the pointed foot through demi-plié in first position to fourth position devant. Straighten the front leg, extending the back foot pointe tendue derrière, and close the back foot in fifth position.

When you first learn pas de Basque, you perform it in a smooth, gliding adagio style. Later you can perform it with tiny jumps in a petit allegro style.

▶ Three-Step Turn

This transition step begins with the working foot pointed devant, the supporting leg in demi-plié. Piqué à la seconde and execute a half turn upstage, ending on both feet in three-quarter relevé; transfer the weight to the other foot and turn a half turn to the front. Step to a full-foot demi-plié à la seconde and point the other foot devant. You can immediately execute the three-step turn to the other side. Learning the three-step turn is preparation for other turning steps such as chaînés.

▶ Chaînés [sheh-NAY] (Linking Turns Like in a Chain)

Begin this series of turns to the right with the right foot piqué à la seconde, or step en relevé followed by a half turn upstage ending with both feet in three-quarter relevé. Then, transfer the weight to the left foot to turn a half turn to the front en relevé to complete one turn. Step out on the right foot en relevé in the direction you are turning and continue this pattern across the space. Transpose the chaînés by starting with the left foot and turning to the left. Practice chaînés across the room from side to side to gain the sense of each half turn. Before adding and coordinating arm movements into the chaînés, practice with your fingertips touching your shoulders.

ALLEGRO

In center combinations, allegro [ah-LAY-groh] steps are fast steps with a brisk, light quality. Most allegro steps include a hop or jump. Collectively these steps are called sautés, or jumps, and are performed by themselves or as part of allegro combinations.

In petit allegro, dancers jump into the air.

Some allegro steps focus on performing small, quick footwork near the floor. This type of footwork is known as **petit allegro**. Other allegro steps focus on performing large hops, leaps, or jumps soaring into the air, or **grand allegro**. Most often grand allegro is executed when moving across the floor.

Performing allegro combinations is both challenging and exhilarating because of the brisk, light, or soaring qualities in the movements. Allegro requires remembering all the movements and their sequence and timing for one step or a series of steps while applying movement principles during quick execution. Scholars consider allegro to be the heart of ballet. To learn a beginning allegro step, practice each step separately and repeat it many times either at the barre or without the barre before combining it with other steps.

Sautés [soh-TAYS] (Jumps)

Sautés, or jumps, are allegro steps and the basis for many petit and grand allegro steps. Sautés include jumps on two legs, hops on one leg, leaps from one leg to the other, and variations. In sautés, begin with a demi-plié in the starting position and propel the body upward into the air; extend the legs and point the feet. Depending on the type of sauté, the legs may change position or direction in the air. The landing technique for all jumps is as important as the takeoff. The landing begins when the toes flex as they reach the floor, pressing through the entire foot and ending in demi-plié. You use counterpull during the landing to appear not to sink and for the landing to be quiet in preparation for the next step or jump.

▶ Coupé [koo-PAY], Devant and Derrière (Cutting Step Front and Back)

Starting in demi-plié in third or fifth position, jump into the air so that both legs fully extend. Then land with either the front foot or the back foot touching the middle of the lower leg. In coupé devant, the side of the little toe touches the front of the leg. In coupé derrière, the heel of the working foot touches the back of the supporting leg.

▶ Sauté [soh-TAY] in First Position (Jump in First Position)

Begin with a demi-plié in first position. Both legs straighten and push into a fully extended first position in the air. Both feet land through toes, metatarsals, then heels into the demi-plié. Use counterpull during the landing. Usually you execute this step in a series of four or eight. It may be combined with other sautés or other petit allegro steps.

▶ Sauté [soh-TAY] in Second Position (Jump in Second Position)

This jump is similar to sauté in first position, but you begin and end in second position. Sauté in second position is executed as a series of four or eight jumps and may be part of a combination of sauté or petit allegro steps.

▶ Changement [shahnzh-MAHN] (Changing Feet)

Starting in third or fifth position, jump vertically. In the air, change the feet from fifth position front through first position to fifth position back. Land in third or fifth position demi-plié with the other foot in front.

▶ Temps Levé [tahm luh-VAY] (Time Raised)

For temps levé, begin jumping from two feet in fifth position with an air moment before ending on one leg with the working foot touching the supporting leg either in front or back, below the knee or in coupé position. The working leg bends at the knee and is turned out. The heel of the working foot touches below the back of the knee.

Temps levé is often incorporated into allegro steps and requires that you jump high enough to completely extend the supporting leg and point the working foot to the floor during the air moment.

▶ Échappé Sauté [ay-sha-PAY soh-TAY] (Escaped Jump)

The échappé sauté lives up to its translation. Beginning in fifth position, jump vertically and open the legs to second position in the air before landing in demi-plié in second position. Jumping from second position, the legs close in fifth position with the other leg in front before landing in demi-plié. The difference between the petit and grand versions of the échappé sauté is the amount of time spent in opening and holding in second position before landing in second position or closing in fifth position.

Petit Allegro Steps [puh-TEE ah-LAY-groh]

The small, quick steps in this category use hops, leaps, and jumps that transfer weight from one foot to the other. Often in the beginning ballet class, these petit allegro steps are practiced independently before they are incorporated into a combination.

▶ Pas de Chat [pah duh shah] (Step of the Cat)

Start in demi-plié in third or fifth position. The back leg lifts to retiré derrière as the front foot pushes into the air. The front leg lifts to retiré devant during the air moment and then both feet land sequentially into demi-plié in third or fifth position.

▶ Jeté [zhuh-TAY] (Thrown)

Beginning in demi-plié in fifth position, transfer the weight to the front leg. Brush the back foot through a full-foot position to à la seconde. The supporting foot pushes the body directly upward into the air. Both legs extend in a small second position before descending. Land on the front foot in demi-plié with the back foot coupé derrière. Ballet vocabulary includes many forms of the jeté step.

▶ Assemblé [a-sahm-BLAY] (Assembled)

Starting in fifth position, the back foot performs a dégagé à la seconde as the supporting leg descends into demi-plié. The supporting foot hops vertically. Both legs close in the air or on the floor in demi-plié in fifth position.

▶ Piqué en Avant [pee-KAY ahn a-VAHN] (Pricked Step Forward)

Begin with the working leg pointe tendue devant. As the supporting leg executes a demi-plié, the working leg lifts to the height of a battement dégagé. The back leg pushes the weight quickly on to the front foot in three-quarter relevé. On relevé, the back heel touches behind the knee. Then the back foot steps into demi-plié directly behind the foot, which releases the front leg and foot into a battement dégagé.

Grand Allegro Steps [grahn ah-LAY-groh]

High jumps and big leaps that soar into the air and land lightly as dancers move across the floor are the hallmark of grand allegro steps. To prepare for grand allegro steps, you use introductory or transitional steps such as walks, runs, chassés, or glissades to help you gain the speed to propel into the air, change direction, or execute another step. In ballet class, you perform these steps either independently or in combinations across the floor. Often these combinations move across the floor near the end of class. Generally, you perform these combinations first in a straight line across the floor and later from corner to corner of the studio on a diagonal.

▶ Arabesque Sauté [a-ra-BESK soh-TAY] (Arabesque Jumped)

The arabesque pose executed with a hop in the air and ending in arabesque en fondu make up this versatile step. The translation of this step is a bit confusing because sauté translates as *jump* and it is really a hop on one leg. To execute this step, step into the arabesque pose and, staying in this pose, demi-plié the supporting leg, hop into the air, and land in a demi-plié. The transitional movements into and out of the arabesque sauté are quick so that the focus is on the beautiful lines of the arabesque. Often you alternate this step from side to side.

▶ Grand Jeté [grahn zhuh-TAY] (Big Leap)

A grand jeté is simply a large leap in which the body travels in an overcurve. The preparation for the grand jeté may be a run, a chassé, or a glissade. As you execute a grand battement devant, the back leg pushes the body into the air and stretches as it rises to 45 degrees or higher. Land on the front leg in demi-plié while the body counterbalances and the back leg stretches upward. The arms move in opposition to the forward leg on the grand battement devant of grand jeté.

Often in the beginning ballet class, after center combinations dancers return to the barre to practice a step. Using the barre to practice a step again helps refine your kinesthetic understanding of the step and areas that might need additional practice.

▶ RÉVÉRENCE

The final part of the center in the traditional ballet class is the révérence [ray-vay-RAHNS], or movement combination to thank the teacher and the musician for dance. This slow movement combination with port de bras is similar for men and women. At the end of the révérence, men bow and women curtsy, then all dancers applaud as they acknowledge the teacher and the musician for dance.

SUMMARY

The center part of the beginning ballet class constitutes learning a basic vocabulary of positions, poses, and different types of steps—the building blocks of ballet combinations and of dances. During your beginning ballet course, simple center combinations get longer and become more complex as they combine various types of movements. These combinations will challenge you physically and mentally. The center is where you learn to dance.

To find supplementary materials for this chapter such as learning activities, e-journaling assignments, and web links, visit the web resource at www.HumanKinetics.com/BeginningBallet1E.

Chapter 8

History of Ballet

Ballet is an art performed around the world today. The history of ballet developed under the patronage of kings for entertainment, impresarios with a calling to present ballet to new audiences, and choreographers and dancers who created new movement ideas to express their artistic visions.

Throughout its history, ballet artists contributed innovations that led to ballet being acknowledged as an independent performing art. Some significant 19th-century ballets survive either through written records or through teaching and staging the ballet for generation after generation of dancers and choreographers. These works represent part of the literature of the ballet as a performing art. *Ballet artists* contributed to changes in ballet styles through their performances of these works. Likewise, the aesthetics of ballet evolved through historical eras and significant works, resulting in a variety of dance styles.

This chapter provides an overview of how ballet has evolved over several hundred years. Knowing about this evolution can help you better understand the movements you perform and the traditions you follow in class. It can also contribute to your enjoyment when viewing ballet performances and help you distinguish between various types and styles of ballet. Knowing how ballet came to be the art form it is today can enhance your overall experience as a ballet dancer.

BEGINNINGS OF BALLET

During the Italian Renaissance, influential dance masters in many of the powerful courts created royal extravaganzas for the aristocracy. Dance masters provided daily instruction to members of the courts in the popular dances of the times and arranged ballet entertainment with both court and professional dancers. Kings, dukes, and the aristocracy commissioned ballets staged in their great halls as part of banquets, entertainment, or outdoor spectacles to celebrate prestigious events such as visiting dignitaries, marriages, and coronations. These ballets used popular social dances of the time and featured poetry, song, music, theatrical machines, and lavish costumes often designed especially for the event.

> **DID YOU KNOW?**
>
> The word *ballet* originated from the Italian *ballare,* meaning to dance. *Ballo* refers to dances performed in the ballroom.

Italian Ballet Moves to France

In the 16th century, Catherine de' Medici (1519-1589) of the powerful Italian de' Medici family married the duke of Orleans, who became King Henry II of France. When she moved to France she brought Italian amusements and entertainments. After Henry's death, Catherine became the regent queen. In this role she commissioned many court ballets, or **ballets de cour**, as politically inspired entertainments. In 1581 the queen commanded Balthasar de Beaujoyeulx, an Italian violinist at court, to produce an extravagant entertainment, **Le Ballet-Comique de la Reine,** which has since become considered the first ballet (figure 8.1). The *Comique de la Reine* became a milestone in ballet history with its innovative geometric formations. The production included dancing, recitation of poetry, music, and lavish scenery and costumes.

Figure 8.1 *Le Ballet-Comique de la Reine.*

The Harvard Theatre Collection, Houghton Library.

In 1588, **Thoinot Arbeau** (ca. 1519-1595) published *Orchesographie,* a book that recorded popular dances of the 16th century. This dance instruction manual included information on dance music, social mores, and marital advice. *Orchesographie* became influential in the transfer of ballet development from Italy to France and important in the development of ballet.

Ballet at the French Court

In 17th-century France, King Louis XIII, an ardent dancer and producer of the court entertainments, often appeared in several performances in one evening with his all-male company. He appeared in a performance at court, another performance at a home of a lesser noble, and a final performance in front of Paris' city hall for townspeople. The king's passion for dancing and entertainment set the stage for the next phase of development of ballet.

Louis XIV

King **Louis XIV** (1638-1715) of France was a dancer, producer of more than 1,000 ballets, and patron of the arts (figure 8.2). Court ballets had predominantly Greek mythology themes and included a combination of dramatic spoken or sung dialog, music, and arranged court dances. Courtiers performed the dances as gods and goddesses or other mythological characters. The dancers wore court dress with added adornments for their roles and masks. Male courtiers or professional dancers performed female roles in the ballets.

Jean Baptiste Lully

King Louis XIV's supervisor of ballets was **Jean Baptiste Lully** (1632-1687), an Italian musician and composer. The court ballets developed into a variety of forms of entertainment. Later appointed the director of the Academie Royale de la Musique, Lully expanded the academy to include dance.

Pierre Beauchamps

A dancer named **Pierre Beauchamps** (1636-1705) later served as the king's dancing master, or maître de ballet. Beauchamps has been credited with refining the number of foot positions into the five positions of the feet, a foundation of ballet technique. As the academy developed, so did dance training and the development of a sophisticated dance technique and performance standards. Professional dancers took the place of courtiers in performing ballets.

Mlle La Fontaine

The first female professional dancer, **Mlle La Fontaine** (1655-1738) appeared in the ballet *Le Triomphe*

Figure 8.2 Louis XIV in the role of le Roi Soleil, The Sun King, 1653.

Bibliotheque nationale de France.

de l'Amour in 1681, performing in a floor-length court dress with high heeled shoes.

Court Dances

During the 17th century, Paris, France, and the Paris Opéra became the center of ballet development. Dances performed at court for social amusement continued as the basis for entertainments and ballet forms. Courtiers and professional dancers spent their days perfecting their dance technique. Learning to dance was a serious study for members of the aristocracy. How well you danced, your manners, and your understanding of court protocol related directly to your place in society.

Beginning in the Renaissance, dances could be categorized into two distinct types: **Haut (high) dances** featured springing, jumping, and kicking movements. In contrast, **basse (low) dances** used skimming or gliding movements across the floor. Many of the group and couple dances that peasants performed in outdoor celebrations, festivals, and life events became sedate, indoor dances in castle banquet halls. Over several centuries haut and basse types of folk dances evolved into specific regional dances in different countries. While at court, two-part musical and dance suites emerged. Nearly a century later, they expanded into four-part suites.

Two-Part Suite

Beginning in the Renaissance, dance and music forms developed together. First a two-part suite began with a **pavane**, a slow, stately processional dance in 4/4 time. The court dancers paraded in couples or trios around the great hall displaying their attire. Immediately following the pavane was the **galliard**, a lively triple-time couple dance with hops, jumps, and kicks. During the dance the man danced a solo for his partner.

The Four-Part Suite

Around 1620, the two-part suite evolved into the four-part suite. This suite of dances and music included the **allemande**, a couple dance in 4/4 time that replaced the pavane as the first dance. For this slow couple dance, the dancers held one or two hands. The man turned the woman under his arm. The **courante**, the second dance in the suite, came from Italy. It was a dance in 3/4 time in which the dancers did light running steps. The courante was a favorite dance of the French court. The third dance was the **sarabande**. Originally from Spain, it was a lively solo dance. When the sarabande reached the French court it became a sedate processional dance in 3/4 time that was danced well into the 18th century. The final dance of the four-part suite was the **gigue**, a popular dance in triple time featuring fast footwork and performed in many versions. Over the several centuries the four-part suite existed,

DID YOU KNOW?

Historians have written that Queen Elizabeth I of England danced five or more galliards before breakfast.

many court dances appeared and disappeared or the dances were incorporated into forms of ballet entertainment.

Forms of Ballet Entertainment

During the 16th and 17th centuries various forms of ballet entertainment appeared that used the steps from court dances. These amusements at court required large halls or ballrooms for dancing. Pages holding torches stood along the walls to light the large dancing space.

Ballet Masquerade

In this popular form of ballet entertainment, the participants attended the ball in costumes and masks. After several dances and a grand ballet, the dancers unmasked and continued to dance long into the night.

Ballet Pastorale

In this specific type of ballet masquerade, the participants wore rustic costumes or represented satyrs or wood nymphs.

Ballet Melodramatique

A mythology-themed ballet, the ballet melodramatique was a series of music, speaking, and singing interludes. As singing gained more prominence in this ballet form, it led to the development of opera.

Ballet Comique

The ballet comique could have either pastoral or mythological themes. This type of ballet extended Renaissance ideas of revitalizing Greek myths and stories of the gods, through the baroque period.

Ballet de Cour

Beginning in 1620 and extending through the reign of Louis XIV, the ballet de cour was a series of ballet entres, or scenes that included dance and spoken text or singing, but without a unified theme that culminated in a grand ballet. The underlying purpose of the ballet form was to glorify the monarch and distract courtiers from royal politics while educating and impressing the court or citizens who attended. Male professional dancers continued to perform the major roles. Later female courtiers danced roles of nymphs and sorceresses.

BALLET MOVES FROM THE COURT TO THE THEATER

After the death of Louis XIV, France and Europe experienced shifts of economic and political power that radiated into the arts as well. The Paris Opéra, which was established in the 17th century, continued as the center of the ballet world, but this was to change during the early 18th century. Choreographers staged ballets produced at the Paris Opéra and created new works on London stages, in German,

Austrian, and Russian court theaters and opera houses, and in the small theaters in colonial America. French ballet technique and artistic style spread throughout Europe to Russia and the American colonies, finding eager audiences in new theater homes.

During the early part of the 18th century, ballets continued to concentrate on the antics of gods and goddesses. Later in the century, human drama became the central focus of ballets. By the end of the century, spirits flew through the air on wires. Continuing from the previous century, male dancers dominated the stage; however, female dancers' roles increased as did their influence on stage.

Stage decor was a series of painted backgrounds and side panels that moved on and off stage to establish the settings for the ballet. A huge candelabra over the stage and a series of candles or footlights around the front edge of the stage illuminated the dancers.

During the 18th century, ballet experienced many reforms as a consequence of a rapidly developing technique, innovations in costuming and music, and expansion of ballet themes and ideas about choreography.

Two generations of dance families ruled the Paris Opéra as *danseur nobles,* the role of leading dramatic male dancers. In the Vestris family, **Gaetan Vestris** (1729-1808) took the title the God of the Dance and his son, **Auguste Vestris** (1760-1842) ruled the Paris Opéra stage in danseur noble roles. Rivaling the Vestris at the Opéra as dancers and dancing masters, the Gardel brothers, Maximilien (1741-1789) and Pierre (1758-1840), propelled ballets in new directions. Male and female dancers in character and comedic roles explored vertical jumps, multiple turns or pirouettes, and beaten movements.

Costume Changes

In the Paris Opéra ballets, men wore stylized court dress, with a **tonnelet** (an above-the-knee hooped skirt), a wig, a mask, and high-heeled shoes. Women performed in floor length court dresses supported by tight corsets, extended panniers and hoops, tall wigs, and masks. For almost three quarters of the 18th century men and women wore masks as part of their costumes.

Women dancers contributed to reforming ballet through choreography and costume innovations. **Marie Camargo** (1710-1770) was an extraordinary dancer known for her style of quick footwork, little jumps, and steps with beats. She shortened her skirt to above her ankles to display her beaten steps. To make her dazzling footwork easier, she discarded her heeled shoes for flat slippers. Her costume reform required her to wear so-called "precautionary panties" because of her leg extensions and new skirt length.

Ballet rival, **Marie Salle** (1707-1756), danced both in Paris and London. Known for her expressive style of dancing, she was one of the earliest recognized female choreographers. When she danced in the ballet *Pygmallion* (1734), Salle abandoned her tight bodice dress with panniers or large-hooped skirt for a simple muslin dress. She created further scandal by removing her wig and wearing her hair down.

Music and Dance Revolutions

Lully's musical style continued into the 18th century with themed evening-long entertainments that contained a series of opera and dance scenes, or **opéra-ballets**. When composer Jean-Philippe Rameau emerged as a musical force, a battle ensued between his views and Lully's well-entrenched form and style. Rameau believed in a dramatic basis for opéra-ballets and music to accompany the dances for a more cohesive performance. In addition to musicians, choreographers and dancers chose sides. Camargo was a *Lulliest*, while Salle became a *Ramist*. This separation in philosophy fed a continued rivalry between these two dancers. With the new music came changes in choreography.

At court and in society, the upper and middle classes took dance classes. Learning the **minuet,** a complicated couple dance, was imperative for attaining the elegance of movement and manners in the ballroom required by society in the 18th century. During the first half of the 18th century, the minuet became symbolic of the aristocracy and the French court; hence, this period has become known as the age of the minuet. In contrast to the minuet, the contredanse became popular in France, England, and America. The **contredanse** was a lively dance for couples. In two lines, facing each other, a head couple led the couples in a series of steps and figures and then handed off the leadership.

Choreographic Directions

Early in the 18th century, **Raoul Auger Feuillet** (ca. 1675-1730) published *Choreographie,* a self-instruction manual that described dances of the period using symbols to notate the floor patterns and steps to the music. This book was a composite of dances from the previous centuries that included the classic positions of the feet, the turnout of the legs, and the use of the French language to express ballet terminology.

By the middle of the century several choreographers incorporated experiments that grew into new directions for ballet.

Jean Georges Noverre

After choreographing at the royal courts of Europe and on the stages of London, **Jean Georges Noverre** (1727-1810) was appointed by Marie Antoinette as the ballet master at the Paris Opéra. A prolific choreographer, he is credited with creating over 150 ballets. His lasting contribution was his *Lettres sur le Danse et le Ballet* (1760),

> **DID YOU KNOW?**
>
> **Choreographer** derives from Greek and means graphic writer. During the 18th century, the term *choreographer* came into use and replaced earlier terms, such as *dance supervisor* or *arranger,* to mean men who created dances.

which he penned to distinguish ballet as an art form separate from opera and which state four principles as the foundation of *ballet d'action.* He wrote the following:

- Ballet uses technical, dramatic, and expressive movement without the use of words.

- Ballet plots should be central to the dramatic plot or theme in which all solos and other dances contribute or relate to the plot.
- Production elements such as scenery, music, or costumes relate to the plot.
- Pantomime and gestures should be meaningful rather than conventional and meaningless.

Kassing (2007), p. 122.

A new form of ballet, called **ballet d'action**, used dance and pantomime to present a unified, dramatic ballet. In 1770, Noverre's ballet *Médée et Jason* emulated the principles of ballet d'action.

Jean Dauberval

Following in Noverre's footsteps, Jean Dauberval (1742-1816) extended Noverre's and his ideas in his two-act ballet, *La Fille Mal Gardée* (1789). In this comic ballet, nobles and peasants resolve a love triangle. The dances included both folk dance and character movements.

Charles-Louis Didelot

At the end of the century, Charles-Louis Didelot's ballets became a precursor for the next century. Female dancers wore wings on their costumes and spirits flew through the air. Didelot staged his works in Europe before he moved to Russia, where his work established the foundations of Russian ballet.

Throughout the 18th century and especially after the French Revolution, ballet spread throughout Europe, to Russia, and to America through French dancing masters and their choreography.

A CENTURY OF CONTRAST: ROMANTICISM TO CLASSICISM

The 19th century was a century of contrasts in ballet styles from romanticism in the first half to classicism in the latter half. Romanticism emerged first as a literary movement during the second half of the 18th century, and by the early 19th century it became a revolt. In contrast to 18th-century society and arts, romanticism extolled humans their potential and emotional side. In 1820 romanticism emerged and spread through the arts; romantic ballet became a major vehicle for this art style. During the first half of the 1800s, wars and political and economic upheaval throughout Europe led the arts through style changes from romanticism to realism to entertainment. In Russia, ballet had been gaining momentum since the 18th century through the continued influence of French ballet masters' extended visits or relocation. In the last quarter of the 19th century, the classical era of ballet appeared not in Europe but in Russia and under the direction of a French dancer and choreographer.

The Russian Imperial Theatres under czar patronage had the financial backing for producing extravagant ballets, hiring dancers from Europe to perform, teach, and challenge Russian dancers. During the classical era, ballet expanded as independent art, rapidly developed a strong ballet technique, experienced changes in ballet form and style, and supported new theater technology. With these changes in ballet performance, form, and style came a change in aesthetics to support ballet as a classical art form.

In one century, ballet gained its independence from opera and drama, became the vehicle for romantic style in the arts, and attained a classical status as a performing art.

Romantic Ballet

Romanticism was a short-lived artistic style in the 19th century that permeated literature, poetry, music, and ballet. Romantic ballets were immensely popular because this form of theatrical entertainment provided people with an escape from the drudgery of life during the Industrial Revolution. With the rise of romanticism as an artistic style, ballet emerged as an independent performing art.

Roles and Style

While ballets were interludes in either opera or drama during the 18th century, **romantic ballets** were dramatic action stories told through dancing and pantomime in two acts. Act I was set in a faraway place or a time in the distant past. Act II took place in a fantastic world, such as a mysterious forest, an exotic place, or a setting under the sea.

The heroine played a central role in romantic ballets. In the first act she appeared as an innocent young maid with villagers or townspeople in supporting roles. In the second act she was transformed into a supernatural spirit of the air or water or transported to an exotic location. Groups of Wilis, naiads, or other spirits or exotic people danced with her.

Women's onstage roles embodied the romantic ideal of women as delicate beings that men should place on pedestals. Contrasting these ethereal female roles were earthy, sensuous, and strong women who represented the emergent, independent women in various sectors of society such as the arts and education.

On stage, men took roles as nobles or peasants. During the ballets, the main characters became involved in love triangles or unrequited love relationships with either humans or spirits. The male lead danced and partnered with the heroine; they did simple lifts and he supported her in beautiful poses.

Female and male dancing roles propelled the romantic style of ballet. The female dancer captured the romantic illusion as a style when she posed for an instant sur les pointes (on the tips of her toes) in her darned ballet slippers. She skimmed the floor in gliding steps, light jumps, and lifts supported by her male partner. Sometimes women danced the roles of spirits. They flew suspended in the air by wires, only to be caught by their partners. Men performed jumps, leaps, and multiple turns in addition to their primary roles as partners.

The romantic style of ballet embodied a melodramatic story with fantastic elements. Dramatic or exotic theatrical settings and technology created fantastic environments, while music supported the dance, mime, and dramatic action to engage and delight audiences.

Romantic Costumes

Female dancers wore romantic **tutus**. These gauzy dresses with tight bodices had layered midcalf or longer tulle skirts. Pink tights and satin ballet slippers with ribbons that tied around the ankles completed the romantic costume. Often the dancers' tutus had tiny wings attached at the back of the waist. The **ballerinas** wore fresh flower crowns and jewels. Male dancers wore peasant shirts, sometimes with vests or jackets, and knee breeches over their tights and black ballet slippers.

All these stylistic elements packaged together as a romantic ballet made for an unbeatable evening of entertainment and diversion from real-world cares.

Romantic Dancers and Choreographers

Female dancers claimed center stage in romantic ballets while male dancers, who had dominated 18th-century ballets, took supporting roles onstage but continued as choreographers and ballet masters and provided artistic direction. Five female dancers were the ballet stars of the romantic era. Each had her own personality and contributions to this amazing yet short-lived era in ballet.

The *Pas de Quatre* showcased the four divinities of romantic ballet.

Jerome Robbins Dance Division, The New York Public Library for the Performing Arts, Astor, Lenox and Tilden Foundations.

Marie Taglioni

An Italian dancer who was trained by her father, **Marie Taglioni** (1804-1884) embodied the ethereal side of romanticism. Her role as the sylph in the *La Sylphide* (1832) made her a star. In *La Sylphide,* she wore a white romantic costume, pink tights, and satin ballet slippers tied with ribbons around her ankles, which became the style for romantic dancers and fashion for society. In performance her delicate movement, floating quality, and ability to pose for an instant on the tips of her toes captured the romantic spirit. Taglioni danced in the major European theaters, and her final performance was in Russia. Her signature ballet roles were *La Sylphide* and the lead ballerina in the *Pas de Quatre*.

Carlotta Grisi

An Italian dancer who studied at La Scala ballet, **Carlotta Grisi** (1819-1899) became the pupil and dancing partner of choreographer Jules

Perrot. At the Paris Opéra, she danced the lead role in the ballet *Giselle*, which was created by Jean Coralli and Perrot; Théophile Gautier wrote the ballet's scenario for her. As the first *Giselle*, Grisi became one of the most important ballerinas in romantic ballet, performing *Giselle* and other ballets in the major European capitals and Russia. Many believe she was the first ballerina to wear a blocked slipper that enabled her to dance en pointe.

Fanny Cerrito

An Italian dancer who gained success at La Scala, **Fanny Cerrito** (1817-1909) went on to become a star of the London stage. As a pupil and partner to Perrot, she performed many of his ballets during the romantic era and after. Her brilliant technique was applauded throughout Europe and Russia.

Lucille Grahn

Danish ballerina **Lucille Grahn** (1819-1907) danced the title role in *La Sylphide* in Denmark before dancing at the Paris Opéra, in other European capitals, and in Russia. Returning to Denmark, she re-created romantic sylph roles in the developing Royal Danish Ballet under the choreographic direction of August Bournonville. She was known as the "Danish Taglioni."

Fanny Elssler

Trained in Vienna, **Fanny Elssler** (1810-1884) performed throughout Europe before appearing at the Paris Opéra in 1834 as an established star. In 1836 she danced a Spanish character solo, the *Cachuca*, which displayed her fiery temperament and earthy movements. This role contrasted the ethereal roles she danced in romantic ballets. Elssler was an excellent actress and a versatile dancer with a brilliant, strong ballet technique that enabled her to dance en pointe. By 1839 she became the leading ballerina at the Paris Opéra and she was rival to Marie Taglioni. The next year, she embarked on a two-year tour of the United States, which put Elssler in breach of contract with the Opéra. When she returned to Europe, she danced in London and Russia, and she finally retired in Vienna.

Jules Perrot

Jules Perrot (1810-1892), a French dancer who studied with August Vestris, danced as a soloist in London before returning to the Paris Opéra as Taglioni's partner. He left the opera and in Italy he became the teacher and partner of Carlotta Grisi. Perrot is considered the greatest male dancer of the romantic era. As a choreographer and ballet master in London, he applied the theories of Jean-Georges Noverre in his romantic ballets. Perrot's ballets had dramatic plots, believable characters, and dramatic action and mime that carried the plot of the ballet forward. In contrast, his *Pas de Quatre* was a ballet that presented the four leading romantic ballerinas and their dancing styles. During the 1850s Perrot became the ballet master in St. Petersburg's Imperial Theater, where he restaged his ballets and created new works.

August Bournonville

Danish dancer, choreographer, and director **August Bournonville** (1805-1879) was a second-generation dancer. He studied at the Royal Danish Ballet and in Paris, partnering with Taglioni. After Paris, he performed in many European capitals before returning to Denmark. As director of the Royal Danish Ballet, Bournonville staged, choreographed, and produced romantic ballets as part of the company's repertoire, although the romantic era had ended.

Romantic Ballets

Of the many romantic ballets choreographed, only a few survive today. The surviving romantic ballets show the development of this choreographic form and style over this short but important era of 19th-century ballet. Romantic ballets established the independence of ballet as a performing art form from 18th-century opéra-ballet. Major attributes of the romantic ballet form and style include the following:

- The ballet is presented in two acts.
- Act I is often set in a faraway place or time.
- A plot usually involves a love triangle, unrequited love, human emotions, and situations.
- The story is told by characters who perform ballet, folk, or character dance and use pantomime and dramatic action to further the plot.
- Act II is set in a unique setting populated by supernatural beings such as under the sea, in a haunted forest, or in an exotic place.
- Humans and supernatural beings interact to complete the dramatic action of the plot.

Romantic ballet plots used Gothic themes, popularized by writers and novels of the time. Many of the romantic ballets had librettos to present the story as well as support the dance and dramatic action taking place on stage.

The era of romanticism and romantic ballet was short, but it had many far-reaching effects on the development of ballet as an art form. Dancers and choreographers performed romantic ballets across Europe, Russia, and the United States. The elements of romantic ballets were to permeate ballets throughout the century and into the 20th century.

***La Sylphide* (1832)**   Filippo Taglioni choreographed this ballet to showcase his daughter, Marie. It ushered in the era of romantic ballet at the Paris Opéra. *La Sylphide* tells the story of James, a Scottish farmer. On the night before his marriage to Effie, James encounters a sylph that he follows into the woods where he meets a witch, Madge. She gives him a magic shawl so that he can capture the sylph. When James finds the sylph, he puts the shawl over her shoulders and she dies. In the final scene of the ballet, James is sitting in his farmhouse. He hears in the distance the wedding festival for his formerly betrothed to another.

***Giselle* (1841)**   Act I opens in a tiny Gothic village, sometime in the distant past. Giselle, an innocent peasant girl, falls in love with Albrecht, a nobleman disguised as a peasant. Hillarion, a huntsman who is also in love with her, warns Giselle that Albrecht has another identity. Her mother encourages Giselle to marry lest she fulfill the prophecy of unwed maids who die and are doomed to dance for eternity. At a village festival for visiting nobility, Hillarion reveals Albrecht's identity. When Giselle discovers Albrecht is engaged to the daughter of the duke, she goes insane and dies. Giselle is destined to become a Wili, a spirit who dances from dusk to dawn.

The second act begins in a mysterious forest at midnight, where Wilis dance from midnight to dawn. First, Hillarion visits Giselle's grave where he is discovered by the Wilis. Led by their queen, Myrtha, the Wilis make him dance until exhausted and then drive him into the lake. When Albrecht appears, Giselle, now a Wili, tries to protect him by dancing with him and spelling him as they danced through the night. At dawn, the Wilis leave to rest for the next night when their dancing begins again. Albrecht is exhausted and leaves the forest with only his memory of Giselle.

The ballet *Giselle* is considered an archetype of a romantic ballet. It contains the salient elements, style, and aesthetics that imbue this romantic style of ballet. The role of Giselle presents a challenge to ballerinas performing it since the dual role requires impressive technique, acting skills, and a mature sense of style to shift from innocent maid to ethereal spirit.

***Pas de Quatre* (1845)**   The director of His Majesty's Theatre in London persuaded the so-called four divinities of romantic ballet, Marie Taglioni, Carlotta Grisi, Fanny Cerrito, and Lucile Grahn, to perform in a ballet. Choreographed by Jules Perrot, this plotless ballet featured each ballerina's unique talents and style.

***Coppélia* (1870)**   During much of the mid-19th century, Europe was plagued with political upheaval and economic events that brought with it a new sense of reality in people's lives and on the stage, too. The ballet *Coppélia* acts as a bridge from romantic to classical ballet. Choreographer Arthur St. Leon (1821-1870), a multitalented dancer, musician, and ballet master, performed in London, throughout Europe, and in Russia. The ballet scenario of *Coppélia*, based on a story by E.T.A. Hoffman, tells the story of Franz and Swanilda and their friends. Dr. Coppélius is a doll maker who creates Coppélia, a mechanical doll. Franz sees Coppélia and, believing she is alive, falls in love with her. Later Franz and Swanilda reunite in the third act of the ballet and celebrate their marriage. Coppélia is a delightful ballet still performed today. It contains many romantic and fantastic elements.

Classical Ballet

During the last quarter of the 19th century, classical ballet emerged in Russia. The classical form emerged from a melding of French dance masters who had restaged their ballets when they visited or relocated to Russia over several centuries, the development of Russian dancers, and lastly, the influx of Italian dance masters and Italian-trained dancers to the imperial Russian ballet. Around the middle of the 19th century, romantic dance artist and choreographer Jean Perrot restaged ballets such as *Giselle* and his other works in Russia. Under Perrot's artistic direction, Marius Petipa, a French dancer, came to Russia to perform. Arthur St. Leon succeeded Perrot as ballet master. After St. Leon, Petipa, who was Perrot's assistant, became ballet master and choreographer in St. Petersburg's Imperial Theatres and considered the architect of classical ballet.

In the late 19th century, ballet reached its classical period as a performing art because of a number of contributing factors: It was financially endowed by royalty, ballets were well-designed choreographic and dramatic theatrical forms, and dancers had reached new levels in their technique and performance.

Classical ballets told dramatic stories that often mixed elements of history, realism, fantasy, and spectacle. The classical ballet ranged from two acts such as the *Nutcracker* (1892), to four acts such as *Swan Lake* (1895), or longer such as *Sleeping Beauty* (1890) that includes an epilogue. These evening-long story-based ballets featured ballet, mime, character dance, and the pas de deux.

In classical ballet, as in romantic ballet, the ballerina reigned supreme onstage, supported by a male **premier danseur**, a hierarchy of soloists, and a **corps de ballet**. Ballerinas and soloists mastered dancing sur les pointes in pointe shoes and executed multiple turns, extended balances, and rapid, intricate footwork. Male dancers stretched ballet technique to new heights as premier danseurs by executing high, gravity-defying leaps and jumps, multiple turns, and astounding beaten steps while they seemed to hang in the air.

Classical Pas de Deux

During the ballet, the premier danseur and the ballerina executed solos and one or more **pas de deux**, or dance for two. The pas de deux challenges the male and female lead dancers' technique, virtuosity, and style. The basis for the pas de deux began in romantic ballet and solidified during the classical era. Some pas de deux have survived while the ballets from which they originated have vanished into history. The highlight of the classical ballet was the **grand pas de deux** performed by the ballerina and the premier danseur. It is the dance that showcases each dancer's ballet technique and artistry as dancers in the leading roles in the ballet.

The pas de deux form, which began in romantic ballets, evolved by the classical era into a dance with four variations. The opening dance or variation was an adagio, or slow, section in which the male and female dancers introduced themselves to the audience as the leading characters in the ballet. The male dancer supports the female dancer in poses and multiple turns. He lifts or carries her in different positions or poses. Following the adagio section are male and female variations. The second dance displays the premier danseur's virtuosity of his beaten steps, gravity-defying leaps, and multiple turns. In the third variation, the ballerina exhibits her technical skills of quick footwork, turns, and balances sur les pointes. In the last variation of the pas de deux, or finale, the two dancers alternate performing short dance sections with even more astounding technical feats and build to a climactic ending. Most romantic and classical ballets have passed into history, leaving only some significant works and pas de deux to be still performed today.

Classical Costumes

Dancers in classical ballets wore a range of stylized costumes to depict their roles. Costumes could convey a historical time, a country, or a fantastic place and add visual attraction to the ballet. In contrast, female soloists and the ballerina most often wore a highly stylized costume, or tutu. Like the romantic tutu, the classical tutu had a tight bodice, but the length of the multilayered skirt varied from midcalf to above the knees to show the dancer's technique and pointe work.

Men's costumes changed little during the 19th century. Premier and soloist male dancers wore elaborately designed costumes to represent a character or status in society and to distinguish them as leading dancers. Male dancers wore knee breeches and tights similar to earlier in the century or tunics with shorter pants and tights.

The Ballet Company

Performing these ballet spectacles required a huge cast of dancers. The hierarchy of dancers ranged from the corps de ballet, or a large group of dancers, upward in status to demi-character dancers, who performed comic or character roles, to soloists. Within the ranks of soloists, the premier danseur and ballerina danced the leading roles in the ballet.

Literally translated, *corps de ballet* means the body of the ballet. This is the large number of dancers who performed group dances as entertainment, to establish atmosphere, present ballet interludes, or perform character dances. **Character dances** blended folk dances and ballet technique into a stylized dance form to represent dances of various cultures. Between the corps de ballet and the soloist ranks, demi-character dancers performed comic or character roles.

Male and female soloists performed short dances throughout the ballet to give the premier danseur and ballerina time to rest. The leading premier danseur and the ballerina performed solos, duets, or pas de deux, and they mimed the dramatic action of the ballet.

Classical Choreographers and Dancers

The Imperial Russian Theatre system included a number of theaters; the most important were the Bolshoi in Moscow and the Maryinsky Theatre in St. Petersburg. At the Maryinsky, ballet crystallized into a classic form. Ballet masters and dancers from Europe since the 1700s had visited or relocated to Russia. During the 19th century, some of the major innovators, both from Europe and Russia, contributed to the development of Russian ballet, choreography, and the classical era of ballet.

Marius Petipa

Marius Petipa (1819-1910) came from a dance family, studying first with his father and then with Auguste Vestris. In the 1840s, he became a principal dancer at the Paris Opéra before moving to St. Petersburg as a dancer, assistant to Perrot, and then ballet master. Petipa created over 50 ballets during his career at the Imperial Theatre. Some of his classical works that survived include *The Sleeping Beauty* (1890), the pas de deux from *Don Quixote* (1869), and *Swan Lake* (with Lev Ivanov; 1895).

His lavish ballet productions extended to evening-long entertainment featuring ballet, mime, and character dances. During this period, female dancers imported from Italy challenged developing Russian dancers' technique. This combination of Italian and French ballet in Russia led to the solidification of the Russian ballet.

Lev Ivanov

A Russian dancer and choreographer, **Lev Ivanov** (1834-1901) studied and performed in Moscow before joining the Maryinski Theatre in 1850. Ivanov worked in the shadow of Petipa until he became ill. Ivanov choreographed the *Nutcracker,* a perennial favorite. His legacy is the second and fourth acts of *Swan Lake.*

Enrico Cecchetti

Italian dancer, mime, and teacher, **Enrico Cecchetti's** (1850-1928) career is largely associated with the Russian ballet. His teaching career spans from Petipa and into the 20th century under Diaghilev. Cecchetti is best known as a teacher to the stars of the Russian ballet and author of a progressive ballet curriculum.

Italian Ballerinas in Russia

While Russian dancers emerged as performing artists in ballet, an influx of Italian ballerinas trained at La Scala and then by Cecchetti performed in the Maryinski Theatre productions.

Pierina Legnani (1863-1923) was born in Milan and danced at La Scala. She astounded London audiences by executing 32 *fouettés en tournant,* or whipping, continuous turns. The following year she danced the leading role in *Swan Lake* at the Maryinski Theatre, performing her famous *fouetté* turns in the ballet. She became an inspiration for Russian dancers to emulate her technical feats, and her work created a new standard for the ballerina in the classical era.

Italian dancer **Virginia Zucchi** (1847-1930) came to perform with the St. Petersburg ballet. A technical virtuoso dancer with superb acting skills, she challenged Russian dancers during the classical era and into the next generation.

Classical Ballets

Classical ballets produced at the end of the 19th century have continued to delight audiences into the 21st century. These ballets are one form of dance literature, similar to music literature from various periods. The classical ballets' form and productions make them unique works with identifying characteristics; in other words, they are classics.

***The Sleeping Beauty* (1890)**   Still performed today, *The Sleeping Beauty* ballet is based on the French fairy tale by Charles Perrault. In collaboration with composer Peter Tchaikovsky, Petipa created this ballet, which was considered the high point of 19th-century czarist Russian culture. The ballet includes some of Petipa's greatest choreographic ideas presented in solo variations, character dances, and pas de deux. Often instead of the entire ballet, either act III or the grand pas de deux is performed today.

The Nutcracker **(1892)**   Petipa wrote the scenario for *The Nutcracker,* but Ivanov choreographed this popular December ballet performed today in many versions. A ballet in two acts, it begins at a Christmas party where Clara receives a nutcracker doll that changes into a handsome prince. He takes her on a dream journey. In act II they arrive in the Land of the Sweets and are welcomed by the Sugar Plum Fairy to a celebration of dancing.

Swan Lake **(1895)**   *Swan Lake* is the prototype of a classical ballet. Petipa choreographed acts I and III set in the palace, while Ivanov choreographed acts II and IV at the lakeside. The ballet tells the story of Princess Odette, who has been turned into a swan by the evil magician von Rothbart. At midnight, the Swan Queen and her swan companions dance. She falls in love with Prince Siegfried, who claims unconditional love but later is unfaithful. In act III, von Rothbarth conjures up Odile, the Black Swan. She captivates the prince, who asks her to marry him. Siegfried realizes he has broken his promise to Odette, and in act IV he rushes to the lakeside to tell her of his unfaithfulness. The ending of the ballet may vary; sometimes it is a happy ending and sometimes it is a sad ending. During the 20th century, a one-act version of *Swan Lake* capsulized the story. Likewise, two beautiful pas de deux are performed as separate works: the act II White Swan pas de deux for Siegfried and the Swan Princess Odette and the act III Black Swan pas de deux for Siegfried and Odile, the Black Swan.

At the end of the 19th century, ballet in Russia had developed and become recognized as a performing art because of new heights of the artists' technique, choreographic geniuses, and royal support of ballet. Meanwhile during the 18th and 19th centuries in the United States, ballet was being transplanted from European sources as roots for future development in the 20th century.

BALLET IN THE UNITED STATES BEFORE 1900

From colonial times through the end of the 19th century, ballet dancers and choreographers found adventure and some even found fortune either through visiting or relocating to the United States. Beginning in colonial times, English theatrical companies toured major eastern coastal cities to perform. These stock companies were small groups of versatile performers who acted, sang, and danced. The performers presented entertainment from circus acts to theatrical evenings with their renditions of great dramas, operas, and the latest popular dances from Europe. During the 18th century, dancing masters from France and other European nations made the long ocean voyage to the United States. They found work in the theaters and communities and taught dance, music, and fencing at some of the early universities.

By the early 19th century, most cities east of the Mississippi River had an opera house, a theater, or other hall for circuses, concerts, or theatrical productions. As the boundaries of the United States moved westward, so did theatrical entrepreneurs. During the 1840s, with the invention of steam boats and extended river travel, dancers and theatrical families of performers extended their tours westward to cities along the major rivers in the eastern United States and up and down the

Mississippi. The transcontinental railroad from St. Louis to the west coast provided a way for theatrical companies to perform on different routes or circuits in cities and towns across the west. In the first half of the 19th century, an evening's theatrical fare was a mixture of drama and melodrama, opera, ballet, and music. During the latter part of the century minstrel shows, musical spectacles, vaudeville, and other theatrical fare entertained audiences with drama, music, and dance.

Dancers

Colonial and early American dancers had to be versatile. Many had trained in ballet, but they performed in a wide variety of entertainment forms and environments including theaters, opera houses, circuses, amphitheaters, and concert halls. Several colonial and American dancers emerged who contributed to the development of ballet in the United States.

John Durang

Known as the first American dancer to receive acclaim, **John Durang** (1768-1822) performed in circuses and opera houses. He gained fame from dancing the horn-pipe, which some consider a forerunner of tap dancing. In 1767, he performed the role of Harlequin Friday in the ballet pantomime *Robinson Crusoe*. Popular in both England and the United States, a ballet pantomime told a story though pantomime and dances.

Augusta Maywood

The first American ballerina, **Augusta Maywood** (1825-1870), trained and made her debut in Philadelphia but spent much of her professional career in Paris, Lisbon, and Vienna, and she became a prima ballerina at La Scala in Milan. She appeared in New York in the Americanized version of *La Sylphide* titled *The Mountain Sylph*.

Mary Ann Lee

The first American *Giselle,* **Mary Ann Lee** (1823-1899) trained in Philadelphia with her contemporary Augusta Maywood. Although Lee performed in Europe, she and her partner, George Washington Smith, formed a small American ballet troupe and toured cities as far west as St. Louis.

George Washington Smith

George Washington Smith (1820-1899) had a long career as a dancer and ballet master. In the 1840s he joined Fanny Elssler's company for its United States tour. In 1846, Smith was the first American dancer to perform the role of Albrecht in *Giselle*. Later in his career he toured the United States with the Italian Ronzani ballet.

Marie Bonfanti

Italian-born ballerina **Marie Bonfanti** (1845-1921) danced in Paris and London before starring as the prima ballerina in *The Black Crook* in 1866, a musical extrava-ganza that premiered in New York and toured nationally. After the production closed, Bonfanti returned to New York to star in the next extravaganza, *The White Fawn*.

Ballets and Entertainments

During the 18th and 19th centuries in the United States, ballets and dances appeared in a range of theatrical fare, operatic performances, and entertainment such as vaudeville shows. Examples include the following:

- *An Allegorical Feast in Honor of the Brave Heroes* was a pantomime ballet to celebrate the American heroes in 1774. Characters included Lady Liberty and American characters such as George Washington and Ben Franklin.
- *Le Foret Noire* (1794), originally produced in Paris, was the first serious ballet presented in the United States.

In 19th-century ballets often women would dance male roles or men would dance female roles, called performing *en travesti*. Sometimes en travesti was done as a novelty, as when a prominent male dancer, who weighed almost 300 pounds, performed the female dancer role in a comic rendition of *Le Dieux et la Bayadère* titled *Buy It Dear, 'Tis Made of Cashmere.* Playing en travesti was often a necessity because male dancers were scarce, so women danced male roles. Female dancers dressed in men's costumes, which showed off their legs clad in tights.

Although women were epitomized in much of the 19th century as delicate creatures, the antithesis was the Amazon woman. These strong female warriors wore armored bodices, short skirts, and tights. The dancers performed sharp, synchronized movements as a group in intricate floor patterns such as in *The Black Crook* and other musical extravaganzas.

In the last half of the 19th century, vaudeville offered another venue for ballet. Tony Pastor, a dancer and showman, opened an Opera House in New York. He rendered the variety show to make it clean family entertainment. As part of vaudeville theatrical fare, female dancers and ballerinas, mostly from Europe, with corps de ballet graced the stage performing skirt dances, fancy dances, and short ballets. When the new century arrived, underlying political and arts movements began to surface to change ballet.

BALLET IN THE 20TH CENTURY

At the turn of the 20th century, classical ballet produced by the Russian Imperial Theatre began to change as the next generations of choreographers and dancers claimed center stage as innovators with new directions. In the first decades of the century, Russian dancers and choreographers extended their influence by performing beyond Western Europe, to the Americas, and across the globe. Wars and political uprisings stimulated Russian ballet dancers' and choreographers' immigration to Western Europe and America, where their work became the roots of ballet in the 20th century. In England, Europe, America, and around the world ballet companies emerged from these Russian artists and teachers from where new generations of choreographers and dancers expressed their ideas, told contemporary stories, and experimented with new styles of ballet for audiences.

The second half of the century explored story and nonstory, or abstract, ballets. These experiments took new directions with the amalgamation of modern dance and other dance forms into ballet choreography. A new generation of choreographers presented personal choreographic ideas to capture contemporary styles and messages of the times and to attract new audiences. In contrast, companies and choreographers retained some of the great works of the romantic and classical eras to keep ballet cultural heritage alive. In the last decade of the century, ballet companies performed modern dance works as well as contemporary ballets and selections from romantic and classical repertories.

The Diaghilev Era of Ballet

In the first decade of the 20th century, while the Imperial Theatres continued to produce classical ballets, **Sergei Diaghilev** (1872-1929), an entrepreneur and theater director, had a vision of showing the best of Russian ballet in theaters of Western Europe and America. After successful exhibitions of Russian art and opera in Paris, Diaghilev selected an artistic team and all-star troupe of dancers from the imperial ranks and organized a company to perform a season of Russian ballets. The 1909 Paris season began Diaghilev's ambition to astound audiences as an avant-garde force in the arts throughout Western Europe, the United States, and South America. Diaghilev gathered premier artists to create ballet productions that presented a total theatrical experience through design of costumes and scenery, contemporary music, and other arts. He personally encouraged and groomed new choreographers to create these innovative ballets, which were to become the basis for the later development of ballet throughout the world during the century.

Throughout his life, Sergei Diaghilev remained the ambitious entrepreneur and visionary who wanted Western Europe and the Americas to see Russian ballet and new choreographers' works capturing the spirit of the first decades of the 20th century.

Michel Fokine

Russian-born dancer **Michel Fokine** (1880-1942) trained at the Imperial Ballet School and upon graduation joined the Maryinksy Ballet. An excellent dancer and partner of prominent ballerinas, he joined Diaghilev's Ballets Russes as a dancer and choreographer. Fokine's ballets were central to the company's success from 1909 to 1912. His story ballets established ballet as a dramatic form with works such as *Firebird* and *Petrouchka*. In contrast, his signature work, *Les Sylphides*, was an abstract in a romantic style.

Anna Pavlova

Russian-trained **Anna Pavlova** (1881-1931) gained the rank of prima ballerina at the Maryinski Ballet and had danced in Europe before joining the Diaghilev Ballets Russes for its first season. In 1910 she made her first appearance in the United States and partnered with Mikhail Mordkin. The following year, she formed her own company. Pavlova and her company toured the United States and throughout the world to captivate audiences who had never before seen a ballet. Her repertoire included the

---

DID YOU KNOW?

Michel Fokine's ballets exemplified five principles of ballet reform that he wrote in a letter to the *London Times* in 1914 (Kassing 2007, p. 176):

1. Each dance should use new forms of movement suitable to its subject and period.

2. Dance and mime should be used to express dramatic action.

3. Mime should be used only when the ballet's style dictates it; in other cases the dancer's whole body, not only the hands, should be used to communicate.

4. The corps de ballet should be used for plot development and as a means of expression.

5. Ballet reflects the alliance of all the arts involved in it: music, scenery, dancing, and costuming. Music should be a unified composition that is dramatically integrated with the plot.

Fokine's choreography was the testing ground for writing these five principles. His work was the transition from the classicism of Petipa to the emergence of modern ballet.

---

classics and her experimental dances. Her performances inspired dancers, and in the minds of the ballet audiences her name become synonymous with the term *ballerina*.

Vaslav Nijinsky

A graduate of the Imperial Ballet School, **Vaslav Nijinsky** (1890-1950) joined the Diaghilev Ballets Russes for its Paris 1909 season. His impressive soaring leaps in Fokine's ballets left a deep impression on audiences. After Fokine's departure in 1912, Nijinsky assumed the role of choreographer in the company. The first ballet Nijinsky created was *L'Après-Midi d'un Faune* (*Afternoon of a Fawn*), in which he performed the title role. Even for sophisticated Parisian audiences, Nijinsky's unconventional choreography, suggestive costuming, and movements left them outraged. In 1913, Nijinsky choreographed *Le Sacre du Printemps* (*The Rite of Spring*), which tested classically trained dancers to perform new rhythms and techniques. Nijinsky went on to create other avant-garde ballet works. By 1917, Nijinsky became mentally ill and left the company. He spent the remainder of his life in a mental institution. Nijinsky is remembered as a phenomenal dancer and avant-garde choreographer who created a new role for the male dancer in 20th-century ballet.

Diaghilev's Russian ballet artists led ballet in new stylistic directions and expanded audiences through tours to the United States, South America, and Europe. World War I halted the company's touring. With the Bolshevik Revolution in Russia, Diaghilev's dancers decided to settle in Europe, England, the United States, and South America, where they would perform and teach Russian ballet.

Léonide Massine

Léonide Massine (1896-1979) was a dancer and choreographer who studied at the Imperial Ballet School in Moscow. He joined Diaghilev's Ballets Russes in 1913 as a dancer and became the company's chief choreographer. His work *Parade* (1917), in which he collaborated with contemporary musicians and artists, established him as a choreographer. In the 1930s Massine choreographed in Europe and the United States and became director of the Ballet Russe de Monte Carlo. In his career he choreographed over 100 ballets in two styles: story ballets with comic elements and abstract ballets performed to symphonic works.

George Balanchine

George Balanchine (1904-1983), a graduate of the Imperial Russian Theatres and previously a dancer and choreographer with the Diaghilev Ballet Russes, came to the United States in the early 1930s. Lincoln Kirstein, American patron, scholar, and dance historian, invited Balanchine to direct a new School of American Ballet and serve as artistic director and choreographer for the company, the American Ballet. After the company dissolved, Balanchine remained in the United States, continuing to produce ballets and choreograph for the follies and musicals until the end of the 1940s, when the New York City Ballet emerged.

Over Balanchine's career he created more than 400 ballets and has been called the father of American ballet. His artistic focus was abstract, neoclassic style ballets. His landmark work, *Apollo* (*Apollon Musagète*), created in 1926 for the Ballets Russes, began his focus on neoclassic style. *Serenade* (1935) was his first original work in the United States. One of his signature works, *The Four Temperaments* (1946), revealed a new 20th-century American style with its clean, spare lines and athleticism. His choreography and direction for the New York City Ballet became the vehicle for his style.

American Ballet Companies

World War II became an isolating factor for the United States. Male dancers became soldiers and repertoire seemed to shift from Russian classical ballets to new emerging American-rooted themes. Jerome Robbins' *Fancy Free* became the signature piece of the era as a story ballet about three sailors on leave for the evening in New York. Agnes de Mille (1909-1993) created ballets on American themes such as *Rodeo*, which centered on a cowgirl and scenes from the West. The ballet scenes captured riding, roping, and a Saturday night square dance. *Rodeo* was the predecessor for de Mille's later long-running musical theater success, *Oklahoma!*

During the 1930s and 1940s, two major ballet companies arose in New York as the foundation of American ballet, while other ballet companies emerged throughout the nation.

Ballet Theatre

During the 1930s one of Pavlova's partners, Mikhail Mordkin, trained dancers and staged Russian ballets in New York City. One of his students, Lucia Chase of the

Chase banking family, collaborated with Richard Pleasant and Oliver Smith to develop a company, Ballet Theatre. In 1940, Ballet Theatre premiered it first season in New York, advertising the season as the best in Russian ballet. An ambitious premier, the Ballet Theatre featured numerous international choreographers and focused on various styles.

Ballet Russe Companies

In 1933, the Ballet Russe opened in New York City after a successful debut in London. Léonide Massine, the company's ballet master, staged many of the Diaghilev era ballets while contributing original ballets, some based on American themes. From the 1930s until the company disbanded in 1962, the Ballet Russe under various names, managements, and a continuously changing cast of dancers toured the United States, bringing ballet to cities and towns and building an American audience for ballet.

New York City Ballet

After American Ballet folded, Balanchine began developing entire evenings of ballet but in a new style that became known as neoclassicism. His abstract or thematic ballets captured the American spirit of athleticism with an ensemble of dancers dressed often in practice clothes. As artistic director of Ballet Society, which became the New York City Ballet, Balanchine created ballets that ranged from story to predominately abstract ballets or ballets with a theme. **Jerome Robbins** (1918-1998), dancer and choreographer and associate director of New York City Ballet, had a dual career; he created works for the New York City Ballet and Broadway blockbusters such as *West Side Story* and *Fiddler on the Roof.* Robbins' contributions to the New York City Ballet provided contemporary ballets that contrasted, complemented, and extended the company's image.

New Ballet Companies

By the 1960s, both the New York City Ballet and Ballet Theatre toured the United States and began visiting capitals across the world. Ballet Theatre became the American Ballet Theatre (ABT), continuing to present a wide variety of choreographers' works and works from romantic and classical ballet repertory. In that same decade, some new small ballet companies developed.

Joffery Ballet

The Joffery Ballet began as a small company of dancers touring with borrowed costumes in a station wagon. The company separated from the Harkness Ballet, directed by Standard Oil heiress Rebecca Harkness. The ballets created by artistic director Robert Joffery and associate artistic

DID YOU KNOW?

In 1959 at the New York City Ballet, modern dancers Martha Graham and Paul Taylor were invited to dance in *Episodes,* a ballet that contained ballet and modern dance sections. *Episodes* triggered new directions in ballet that had been evolving.

Dancers from the Dance Theatre of Harlem.

director Gerald Arpino explored new subjects, themes, and styles such as pop art and other trendy art styles in the 1960s. To augment this ambitious repertory, Joffery and Arpino tapped earlier 20th-century choreographers and dancers to restage ballets from the first part of the 20th century.

Dance Theatre of Harlem

Arthur Mitchell (1934–), who was the first African American principal dancer with the New York City Ballet, left the company to return to Harlem in 1968. Mitchell had starred in some of the seminal Balanchine works, such as *Agon*. One year later, Mitchell founded the Dance Theatre of Harlem featuring works by Balanchine, revised classics, and contemporary choreography.

Decentralization of Ballet in America

During the second half of the 20th century, ballet companies in U.S. cities that had started in the early part of the century gained prominence nationally and even internationally. The San Francisco Ballet, Pennsylvania Ballet, Atlanta Ballet, Houston Ballet, Chicago Ballet, Pacific Northwest Ballet, Miami Ballet, and other companies presented romantic, classical, and 20th-century ballets, in addition to their individual artistic directors' and choreographers' contemporary repertories. This growth of ballet companies beyond New York in a number of U.S. cities provided new places for audiences to enjoy ballet.

Dancers

American dancers and companies presented repertories of classical and 20th-century ballet works. An influx of Russian ballet stars defecting to the West brought yet another outlook to incorporate into contemporary ballet. Following are descriptions of just a few of the many ballet stars who contributed to the art of ballet during the second half of the 20th century.

Suzanne Farrell

Born in Cincinnati, **Suzanne Farrell** (1945–) graduated from the American School of Ballet, and at 16 she joined the New York City Ballet (NYCB). Her physical attributes captured the essence of a Balanchine dancer and consequently she acquired an extensive Balanchine repertory. She left NYCB to dance in Europe before returning to NYCB in 1975 as partner to artistic director Peter Martins.

Gelsey Kirkland

In 1968, **Gelsey Kirkland** (1952–) joined NYCB. She created many Balanchine and Robbins roles. From 1974 to 1984, she danced with ABT, partnering with Mikhail Baryshnikov.

Rudolf Nureyev

Already a star in the Soviet Union with the Kirov Ballet, **Rudolf Nureyev** (1938-1993) began his Western career when he defected in 1961 while on tour. First dancing in England and then America, he danced and choreographed or restaged ballets with major ballet and modern dance companies. In 1983 he became the director of the Paris Opéra Ballet. Nureyev is considered one of the foremost male dancers of the 20th century.

Mikhail Baryshnikov

A graduate of the Leningrad Choreographic Institute (now the Vaganova Ballet Academy), **Mikhail Baryshnikov** (1948–) joined the Kirov Ballet in 1966. His technical virtuosity accorded him premier danseur roles. In 1974 on tour in Canada with the Stars of Bolshoi Company, Baryshnikov defected. He moved to the United States and joined American Ballet Theatre. In 1978, he joined NYCB and rejoined ABT in 1980. Baryshnikov's performances extend beyond classical and contemporary ballet to modern dance, film, and television. His technical and performance virtuosity make him one of the icons of 20th-century ballet.

Natalia Markarova

A Vaganova Ballet Academy graduate, **Natalia Markarova** (1940–) joined the Kirov Ballet dancing leading roles in classical ballets. In 1971, she defected to the United States and joined American Ballet Theatre. Her performances spanned classical to contemporary ballets. In 1988 she danced her final performance with the Kirov Ballet in London. She has revived and staged many classical and 20th-century ballets for companies around the world.

Next Generation of Ballet

Beginning in the 1970s and during the 1980s, the popular television series *Dance in America* and other dance performance series, made possible by the National Endowment for the Arts and other grants, allowed ballet to be viewed in people's living rooms. The accessibility of ballet had a cyclic effect with increased attendance, arts advocacy, and dance education.

By the last decade of the 20th century, many of the major ballet artists and choreographers passed on. New financial times demanded that ballet companies change to survive. The Joffery Ballet moved their base of operations from New York to Chicago. To support major metropolitan ballet companies' seasons, during the mid-1980s some cities shared their seasons. New dancers, choreographers, and companies made their own statements as they took their place on the American stage. Often these artists' statements blurred the lines further between ballet, modern dance, and other dance forms to present a personal interpretation, a statement, or an aesthetic view.

Eliot Feld

Eliot Feld (1943–) performed on Broadway and was principal dancer at NYCB and ABT before starting his own company. His first company, American Ballet, which began in 1969, has changed names over time. Feld's 100-plus ballets since the late 1960s are eclectic, use music, and combine modern dance with ballet to feature ensemble work.

Alonzo King

A native of Georgia, **Alonzo King** trained in New York and performed with Dance Theatre of Harlem and with other dance artists' companies before establishing his company, Alonzo King LINES Ballet, in San Francisco in 1982. King has created contemporary ballets internationally performed by companies and on television and film.

Karole Armitage

American choreographer **Karole Armitage** (1954–) studied ballet and performed with modern dance choreographer Merce Cunningham. In the early 1980s, she began combining ballet and modern dance to create a new technique, featured in her work *Watteau Duets*. Throughout her career she has toured the United States and Europe with her company. Her work focuses on intense musicality in her choreographic works and collaboration with contemporary artists.

INTERNATIONAL PERSPECTIVES IN THE 20TH CENTURY

The 20th century saw many changes. In the first decade, classical ballet dancers who were trained in Russia astounded Western European, then American and South American, audiences with their dazzling performances. Wars and political changes generated migration of dancers and choreographers from one part of the world to new homes where they performed and taught their art. This constant cross-fertilization of ballet, expansion of choreographic styles, and absorption of other dance forms created a richness of the tapestry of 20th-century ballet.

By the end of the century, ballet was no longer a Western European or American dance form; it was danced, choreographed, and produced worldwide. If you do a quick Internet search, you can find ballet in South America, Africa, Asia, and Australia. To write about ballet, its history, dancers, choreographers, and works in these and other places would take volumes. This is your opportunity to explore ballet around the world or in your community.

VIEWING BALLET PERFORMANCES

Usually a beginning ballet course includes viewing one or more ballet performances. The performance could be a live performance or on video. There is a vast difference between viewing a professional ballet company performing a work and what you are learning in beginning ballet. Likewise, there are many similarities. Professional ballet dancers perform the same barre and center sections of the class that you are learning in beginning class. The difference lies in the complexity of the exercises and combinations.

The range of companies that perform ballet is diverse. You might live in an area where you have the opportunity to see a regional, national, or international company perform a classical or contemporary ballet work. Or a ballet company could be on tour through your community or a nearby city, which presents an opportunity to see a specific company perform. Other times, an opportunity to view a ballet performance may be seeing a local civic ballet or university company perform a ballet as part of their annual season.

When viewing a ballet performance, dancers interpret the choreographer's concept and style into their work. In other words, the dancers contribute to the performance of the choreographer's work with their personal style and artistry.

Etiquette for Viewing a Theater Performance

Part of viewing a dance performance in a theater includes following theater etiquette. If the ballet performance is an afternoon rather than an evening performance, the requirements are more relaxed. However, specific parts are the same, regardless of the time or type of performance.

Before Viewing the Performance

Plan to arrive at the theater usually 30 minutes before the performance to allow yourself time to get your tickets and enjoy the theater's atmosphere as you find your seat. You may have gotten your tickets before the performance. If you pick up tickets at the box office, often they have to be paid for before a certain time, or the box office will be allowed to release them for sale to other parties. So, if you are going downtown for a performance, allow yourself enough time to get to the theater and find a parking space if you drove there.

After you enter the theater and find your seats, enjoy the ambience of a live theatrical performance atmosphere. When the lights dim, the performance begins. When an orchestra is part of the performance, the conductor enters the pit and bows as the audience applauds, then the overture begins. Then, the curtains open and the magic of the performance begins.

During the Ballet

Throughout the performance, dancers perform some extraordinary technical feats, and you may hear audience members clapping. Traditional ballet etiquette is to wait until the act or scene is complete and then applaud. Intermissions are times to get out of your seat and visit the lobby. You may see a flashing of the lights or a musical chime as a signal to remind you when to return to your seat as the intermission is almost over.

After the Performance

At the end of the performance, the cast bows in one or more curtain calls. When the audience has ended its applause, the lights come up in the theater, signaling that it is appropriate to exit.

You can watch a ballet in several ways. Enjoying the movement, the music, and the production as an evening at the theater is obviously foremost. But as a student there are contributing elements of the production that will help you gain a deeper view of the choreography and the choreographer to gain an understanding of the production and ballet as a performing art.

In a ballet, the dancers continue to move through space and time as the dance unfolds before the audience's eyes. Gaining the full effect of a ballet may take watching a performance more than once to understand its meaning or realize its impact. This is no different than listening to a favorite piece of music repeatedly to gain an understanding of the work. Like other arts, ballet is a multisensory experience. When attending a ballet, the movement often connects the audience member in a kinesthetic sense to a dancer and to the dance. When you are absorbed in the dance performance it is easy to sink into watching the moving formations or relationships, but there is more to understand beyond the performance.

Often attending either a live or recorded performance for class includes writing a dance concert report. The web resource includes a dance concert report form outline. Reading the report format before you go to the performance will help you keep in mind some of the things to observe during the ballet. It is not advisable to read the program notes or write the report during the performance. Rather, the main purpose of attending the performance is to enjoy and absorb the experience with your senses. After the ballet is the time to gather the facts, record your impressions, and write the report. You should write your report within 24 hours of the performance, while its imprint is fresh in your mind. When reviewing a ballet, you need to pay attention to several aspects of it.

Understanding the Choreographer's Concept

Understanding a ballet entails seeking the message or theme in the movement. The choreographer is the person who creates the movement to music for the dance. Through dance, movement, and gesture, the choreographer expresses an idea, a statement, a theme, or a story, which is the choreographer's concept for the ballet. This concept could be something personal, a social statement, or a universal affirmation. Ballet vocabulary allows the choreographer to express a concept using a variety of ballet styles that may include other dance forms blended to support the concept.

The choreographer's concept, creativity, and ability in conveying it through movement and relationships to the audience are the essence of ballet. This connection between choreographer and dancers must be innate on many levels in addition to movement. The dancers who receive the movement from the choreographer are the vehicles that express it, so they must have a deep understanding of the content, the message, and the style in which they are expected to communicate the movement to reach audience members.

Members of the audience range from someone seeing a ballet for the first time to someone who has viewed ballet over many years and has built up a mental repertory of ballet works and performers who have danced them. A person with a huge repository can compare and contrast the dancers' technique and performing styles of the work.

Gaining a visual repertory of ballet works and a choreographer's signature works or styles becomes second nature to dance students, dancers, and ballet audiences. Since performance is the vehicle for learning the literature of dance, students, dancers, and connoisseurs of dance continue to attend performances to add to their viewing repertory and knowledge of ballet.

Dancers' Execution (Technique, Style, Performance)

Dancers express thoughts, ideas, and moods through movement, steps, gestures, and facial expression to convey the choreographic concept of the ballet. The dancers' technique can convey various styles of ballet from classical to modern in simple to complex dances. Most often modern ballet styles include varying degrees of modern dance or other dance genres and movements used to convey the choreographer's style or vision for the dance or blending of different dance styles to convey a particular dance theme. Whatever the technique or style, the dancers are the focal point as they perform the dance work. Their performance provides a wealth of information about the dancers' abilities to perform as well as the choreographer's concept, choreographic design, and execution in expressing a central idea to the audience.

Production Elements

The staging of the ballet either in a theater or in another performance space includes support from various production elements, including costumes, lighting, and set design. The production and design elements add visual appeal in a supporting role to the dance. Production elements can set the ballet in a specific time period such as romantic, classical, or contemporary. The elements contribute to creating a complete production that claims the audience's attention and involvement.

Stage Setting

The ballet can be staged in front of only a background or backdrop that eliminates all visual elements to concentrate the focus on the dancers and the dance, or the ballet could be set against a background of a magnificent palace setting, a pastoral scene, or many other painted backgrounds or sculptural settings. The setting establishes place and time and helps establish the ambience for the dance. During the ballet, the dancers may or may not interact with the setting.

Lighting

Lighting design for dance enhances the dancers and the movement and supports the choreographer's concept. Dance lighting is specific to enrich the stage space by depicting a place, time, or mood designed to support the choreographer's concept.

Costumes

Costumes distinguish the dancer's characters, theme, or choreographer's concept for the dance and its style. The dancers' costumes can be elaborate, period, or practice clothes similar to those worn in class. If the latter, the lack of costuming adds focus to the dancers and the movement.

Music

Music in ballet complements or counterpoints the movement. All these elements in a theatrical setting are the makings for a multisensory experience—a feast for the eyes and the ears—and lead to a heightened awareness and involvement with the movement; the audience traces the movement through the work from its beginning to end. As in the movies or even real life, ballet performance includes mystery, suspense, surprise, fear, and joy.

DISTINGUISHING TYPES AND STYLES OF BALLET

After ballet emerged as an art form in the 19th century it continued to keep a story or dramatic plot. Twentieth-century ballet included abstract ballets that focused on moods or themes, ballets with underlying psychological or social perspectives. In the second half of the 20th century, ballet absorbed modern dance and other dance genres to again reinvent itself for contemporary audiences and times. In the 21st century, ballet continues to change styles within and beyond the postmodern era.

Viewing one or more ballets from each of these periods helps you gain a sense of what changed and what remained the same in this performing art. It also helps you to distinguish what types and styles you prefer or might want to discover more about. But similar to trying a new food, sometimes you have to try it a couple of different ways or times to really determine whether you like it or not; the same is true of ballet. Types of ballet include story ballets and abstract ballets, and within this range numerous styles exist. Some historical periods have a stronger focus on one type or style than another.

Story Ballets

A story ballet captures the dramatic action of a story that might have been a fairy tale, a drama, or a folk tale. Dancers portray the major and supporting characters in the story through dance and pantomime. Examples of the story ballets produced today include the following:

- *Giselle,* a romantic ballet
- *Swan Lake,* a classical ballet

Many story ballets span the 19th and 20th centuries.

Abstract Ballets

Although abstract ballets appeared before the 20th century, many ballets throughout the 20th and early 21st century are abstract ballets. In an abstract ballet, the dancers explore the choreographer's concept, which might include embedded or subliminal themes, emotions, universal truths, a personal statement, a style, or a blending of styles. Like an abstract painting, the abstract ballet presents the choreographic artist's distinct point of view. Following are some examples of abstract ballets from the 20th and 21st centuries:

- *Les Sylphides*
- *Agon*, a neoclassical ballet by George Balanchine
- *Aurora I*, a contemporary 20th-century ballet by Eliot Feld
- *Dust and Light*, a 21st-century contemporary ballet by Alonzo King

SUMMARY

Ballet types and styles come and go, but the art of ballet, which started in the Renaissance, continues today as performance and literature of the art form reside in the minds and hearts of dancers and students across the world. The history of ballet for the 21st century remains to be written.

As a performing art ballet responded to historical changes as did other arts. It evolved with social, economic, and political changes of the times yet maintained its identity as a dance and art form throughout the centuries. The history is just one aspect of learning about ballet that can enrich your enjoyment of ballet as a performing art. A beginning ballet class can be the starting place for participating in ballet courses in your future, reading and learning about ballet as an art form, or viewing ballet performance for entertainment or enrichment. Whatever your interest or direction today or in the future, the world of ballet is out there for your enjoyment, education, and exploration.

To find supplementary materials for this chapter such as learning activities, e-journaling assignments, and web links, visit the web resource at www.HumanKinetics.com/BeginningBalletIE.

Glossary

action words—Words that describe body actions (legs, arms, and head movements in the sequence of execution) during an exercise, step, or pose.

active-foot position—Position in which you balance on one foot that supports the weight of the body while the other foot assumes various positions either on the floor, in the air, or resting on the supporting leg.

adagio—Slow, sustained movements and poses. In an adagio combination, you strive to perform positions, poses, and steps with an effortless, smooth quality.

à la quatrième derrière [ah lah ka-tree-EM dehr-YEHR]—Classical body position facing en face with the working leg in the fourth position back.

à la quatrième devant [ah lah ka-tree-EM duh-VAHN]—Classical body position facing en face with the working leg in the fourth position front.

à la seconde [ah lah suh-KOHND]—Classical body position facing en face with the working leg to second position.

alignment—Good dance posture that constantly integrates the dancer's body as a whole—head, torso, arms, and legs—while moving through space or holding a pose, which makes alignment both a static and a dynamic movement principle.

allegro [ah-LAY-groh]—Fast steps with a brisk, light quality. Petit allegro steps include small hops and jumps.

allemande—The first dance of the four-part suite; derived from a slow couple's dance from the 16th century done in 4/4 time. The dancers held one or two hands and the gentleman turned the lady under his arm.

aplomb—Perpendicularly; the ability to appear to move vertically either upward or downward.

arabesque [a-ra-BESK]—A versatile pose with several variations. The dancer balances on one leg and extends the working leg behind at approximately 45 degrees.

arabesque à terre—Arabesque with the working foot pointed and resting on the floor.

arabesque en fondu—Arabesque melted; in this variation of the arabesque pose, the supporting leg is in fondu, or a demi-plié on one leg.

arabesque sauté [a-ra-BESK soh-TAY]—Arabesque jumped or hopped.

Arbeau, Thoinot (ca. 1519-1595)—Published *Orchesographie* (1588), a book that recorded popular dances of the 16th century.

Armitage, Karole (1954–)—American dancer who studied ballet and performed with modern dance choreographer Merce Cunningham. In the early 1980s, she began combining ballet and modern dance to create a new technique featured in her work *Watteau Duets*.

artistry—Ability of a dancer to express ballet movement using fluidity, grace, style, and a performance attitude.

assemblé [a-sahm-BLAY]—Assembled. Starting in third or fifth position, the back foot performs a dégagé or jeté à la seconde as the supporting leg descends into demi-plié. The supporting foot hops vertically. Both legs close in the air or on the floor in a demi-plié in third or fifth position.

à terre [ah tehr]—On the floor; refers to movements performed with the working leg touching the floor as opposed to in the air.

B+ (attitude derrière pointe tendue à terre)—Standing on one foot, the back leg bends at the knee with the foot pointed and the tip of the great toe touching the floor. The B+ position is an alternative beginning position to fifth position for combinations in the center or across the floor.

balance—The principle that you use to continually readjust the alignment of body parts to one another in a pose or while moving.

balancé [ba-lahn-SAY]—Rocking step; the balancé can be performed slowly (adagio) or briskly (allegro), both side to side and front and back.

Balanchine, George (1904-1983)—A graduate of the Imperial Russian Theatre and a dancer and choreographer with the Diaghilev Ballets Russes. He came to the United States in the early 1930s. Balanchine directed a new School of American Ballet and served as artistic director and choreographer for the American Ballet Company. He continued to produce ballets and choreographed for the follies and musicals until the establishment of the New York City Ballet. He created more than 400 ballets and has been called the father of American ballet. His artistic focus was an abstract neoclassical style of ballet. His landmark work, *Apollo* (*Apollon Musagète*, 1926), focused initially on neoclassical style. *Serenade* (1935) and *The Four Temperaments*

(1946) revealed a new American style of ballet with clean, spare lines and athleticism.

ballerina—The leading female dancer who performs solos, duets, or pas de deux and mimes the dramatic action of the ballet.

ballet—Originated from the Italian word *ballare*, meaning *to dance*; a Western classical dance form and one of the performing arts.

ballet d'action—A form of ballet that used dance and pantomime to present a unified, dramatic ballet. Noverre wrote about the four basic principles of ballet d'action in his *Lettres sur le Danse et le Ballet* (1760).

ballets de cour—Court ballets performed in the 16th and 17th centuries.

ballet technique—Comprises a vocabulary of exercises, steps, positions, and poses.

ballet walk—An articulated way of walking in ballet, stepping through each foot from the toes to the heels in a turned-out position.

barre—A series of exercises to warm up and strengthen the body as preparation for the center part of class. The barre is a wooden or metal rail attached to several walls of the studio, or it may be a free-standing portable structure placed in the center of the studio.

Baryshnikov, Mikhail (1948–)—A graduate of the Leningrad Choreographic Institute (now the Vaganova Ballet Academy). He joined the Kirov Ballet in 1966. In 1974 on tour in Canada with the Stars of Bolshoi Company, Baryshnikov defected. He moved to the United States and performed with American Ballet Theatre and New York City Ballet. His performances extend beyond classical and contemporary ballet to modern dance, film, and TV. His virtuosity and technique and performance make him one of the icons of 20th-century ballet.

basse (low) dances—Court dances from the 15th and 16th centuries that contained skimming or gliding movements across the floor.

battement dégagé en cloche [bat-MAHN day-ga-ZHAY ahn klawsh]—Disengaged beating while swinging like a clapper in a bell.

battement dégagé or jeté [bat-MAHN day-ga-ZHAY or zhuh-TAY]—Battement disengaged (dégagé) from (Cecchetti) or thrown (jeté) from the floor (Russian).

battement développé [bat-MAHN dayv-law-PAY]—Unfolding of the leg.

battement frappé [bat-MAHN fra-PAY]—Beating of the foot by striking the floor.

battement tendu [bat-MAHN than-DEW]—A stretched beating.

battement tendu en promenade [bat-MAHN than-DEW ahn prohm-NAHD]—A series of battements tendus à la seconde executed with alternating feet, closing in the starting position. The *en promenade* refers to walking backward or forward.

battement tendu jeté pointe [bat-MAHN than-DEW zhuh-TAY pwen-TAY]—See *petit battement piqué.*

battement tendu relevé [bat-MAHN than-DEW ruhl-VAY]—Battement tendu stretched and raised.

battement tendu with demi-plié [bat-MAHN than-DEW with duh-MEE plee-AY]—A stretched beating with half bend.

Beauchamps, Pierre (1636-1705)—Dancer who served as King Louis XIV's dancing master, or maître de ballet. Beauchamps has been credited with refining the five positions of the feet, a foundation of ballet technique.

Bonfanti, Marie (1845-1921)—Italian-born ballerina who danced in Paris and London before starring as the prima ballerina in *The Black Crook* in 1866, a musical extravaganza that premiered in New York.

Bournonville, August (1805-1879)—Danish dancer, choreographer, and director who was a second-generation dancer. He studied at the Royal Danish Ballet and in Paris, partnering with Taglioni. He performed in many European capitals before returning to Denmark. As director of the Royal Danish Ballet, Bournonville staged, choreographed, and produced romantic ballets as part of the company's repertoire, although the romantic era had ended.

bowlegs—When a space exists between the knees when standing with the insides of the feet together.

Camargo, Marie (1710-1770)—An extraordinary dancer known for her style of quick footwork, little jumps, and steps with beats. She shortened her skirt above her ankles to display her beaten steps. To make her dazzling footwork easier, she discarded her heeled shoes for flat slippers.

Cecchetti, Enrico (1850-1928)—Italian dancer, mime, and teacher whose career is largely associated with the Russian ballet. His teaching career spans from Petipa into the 20th century under Diaghilev. Cecchetti is best known as a teacher to the stars of the Russian ballet and author of a progressive ballet curriculum.

center—Part of the beginning ballet class in which students learn steps, positions, poses, and combinations to gain a basic movement vocabulary of ballet.

center barre—Also called *center practice*, it is one or more exercises learned at the barre and practiced in the center.

center line—Vertical line down the front of the body that divides it into two halves.

Cerrito, Fanny (1817-1909)—Italian dancer who became a star of the London stage. As a pupil and partner to Perrot, she performed many of his ballets during the romantic era and after. Her brilliant technique was lauded throughout Europe and Russia.

chaînés [sheh-NAY]—Linking turns, as in a chain.

changement [shahnzh-MAHN]—Changing feet; refers to a jump in which you start in third or fifth position, jump into the air with legs extended in first position, and change to the other leg in front in third or fifth position in the descent.

character dances—In the 19th century, a blending of folk dances and ballet technique to represent a stylized dance form of various cultures.

chassé à la seconde [sha-SAY ah lah suh-KOHND]—Chasing step in second position. This versatile step can be executed in various directions, such as chassé devant.

chassé devant [sha-SAY duh-VAHN]—Chasing step front. The closing part of the step comes from the quick push from the back leg for the air moment.

choreographer—Derived from the Greek word meaning graphic writer; the creator of a dance work. During the 18th century, the term replaced earlier terms such as *dance supervisor* or *arranger*.

classical ballets—Ballets produced during the last quarter of the 19th century in Russia that told dramatic or fantastic stories. Classical ballet ranged from two acts to four acts or longer. These evening-long events featured ballet, mime, character dance, and the *pas de deux*.

classical positions of the body—Eight basic positions that can be performed as a combination in itself or incorporated with other steps into combinations.

contredanse (also contradance)—A lively dance for couples, especially popular during the second half of the 18th century. In two lines facing each other, a head couple led the couples in a series of steps and figures and then handed off the leadership.

corps de ballet—Literally, the body of the ballet. A large number of dancers who performed group dances as entertainment, to establish atmosphere, or to present ballet interludes.

counterbalance—When the torso tilts upward stretching on a slightly forward angle.

counterpull—The oppositional lift to prevent the body giving into gravity.

coupé [koo-PAY]—Literally, cut; sometimes referred to as low retiré.

coupé devant and derrière—Cutting step front and back. Starting in third or fifth position, demi-plié, then jump into the air so that both legs fully extend. Land with either the front foot or back foot touching the middle of the lower leg. In coupé devant, the side of the little toe touches the front of the leg. In coupé derrière, the heel of the working foot touches the back of the supporting leg.

courante—The second dance in the two-part suite; a dance in 3/4 time in which the dancers did light running steps.

croisé derrière [kwah-ZAY dehr-YEHR]—Crossed in the back. In this classical body position the body faces a downstage corner with the upstage, working leg extending back to the opposite, upstage corner. Arms and head depend on the method or school.

croisé devant [kwah-ZAY duh-VAHN]—Crossed in the front. In this classical body position the body faces a downstage corner, and the downstage leg is crossed in front of the supporting leg. Arms and head depend on the method or school.

dancer stage directions—Relate to the walls and corners of the dance space, which could be the dance studio or another performance space, such as a stage. Russian and Cecchetti methods use different numbering systems for dancer stage directions.

demi-plié [duh-MEE plee-AY]—Half bend of the knees.

demi-seconde position (or half-second)—The arms stretch at half the height between second position and fifth position en bas.

derrière—To the back.

devant—To the front.

Diaghilev, Sergei (1872-1929)—Russian entrepreneur and theater director who created the Ballets Russes company that toured Europe and North and South America, bringing early 20th-century ballets to new audiences.

Durang, John (1768-1822)—First American dancer to receive acclaim performing in circuses to opera houses. He gained fame from dancing the hornpipe. In 1767, he performed the role of Harlequin Friday in the ballet pantomime *Robinson Crusoe*.

écarté devant [ay-kar-TAY duh-VAHN]—Separated, thrown wide apart. In this classical body position the body faces a downstage corner, the working leg stretches to the opposite downstage corner, the downstage arm is overhead, and the upstage arm is in second position.

échappé sauté [ay-sha-PAY soh-TAY]—Escaped jump. Beginning in first, third, or fifth position, jump vertically and open the legs to second position in the air before landing in demi-plié. Jumping from second position, the legs close in first, third, or fifth position, closing the other leg in front before landing in demi-plié.

effacé devant [eh-fa-SAY duh-VAHN]—Shaded, front. In this classical body position, the body faces a downstage corner and the working leg stretches devant to that same corner. Arms and head depend on the method or school.

Elssler, Fanny (1810-1884)—Trained in Vienna. She performed throughout Europe before appearing at the Paris Opéra in 1834 as an established star. In 1836 she danced a Spanish character solo, *La Cachuca*, which displayed her fiery temperament and earthy movements and became her signature role. Elssler was an excellent actress and a versatile dancer with a brilliant, strong ballet technique that enabled her to dance on pointe. By 1839 she became the leading ballerina at the Paris Opéra and rival to Marie Taglioni. The next year, she embarked on a two-year tour of the United States. When she returned to Europe, she danced in London and Russia and then retired in Vienna.

en arrière—Backward.

en avant—Forward.

en croix—Pattern in the shape of a cross.

en face—Facing fully toward the front toward the audience or the front of the room in the studio.

en l'air [ahn lehr]—In the air; refers to the position of the working foot.

épaulé [ay-poh-LAY]—Shouldered. In this classical body position the body faces a downstage corner, and the downstage working leg extends behind to the opposite upstage corner; the downstage arm extends forward at eye level; the upstage arm extends behind. The torso twists upstage so that the arms create a complete diagonal line. The head lifts and tilts to the right or upstage. The eyes focus on the fingertips of the forward hand.

Farrell, Suzanne (1945–)—Born in Cincinnati, she graduated from the American School of Ballet. At 16 she joined the New York City Ballet. Her physical attributes captured the essence of a Balanchine dancer and consequently she acquired an extensive Balanchine repertory.

Feld, Eliot (1943–)—Performed on Broadway and was principal dancer at New York City Ballet and American Ballet Theatre before starting his own company, the American Ballet Company, in 1969. Feld's more than 100 ballets are eclectic, use music, and combine modern dance with ballet to feature ensemble work.

Feuillet, Raoul Auger (ca. 1675-1730)—Published *Choreographie*, an instruction manual, which described dances of the period using symbols to notate the floor patterns and steps to the music.

fifth arabesque (Cecchetti)—The body faces a downstage corner; the supporting leg is the downstage leg in a demi-plié. The arms are the same as for third arabesque. The head tilts upstage and the eyes focus toward the downstage corner.

fifth position (feet)—The heel of the front foot touches the back foot. In the Vaganova method, the heel touches the tip of the toe of the back foot. In the Cecchetti method, the heel touches the back foot at the joint of the great toe.

fifth position en haut—Rounding both arms high, diagonally upward from the hairline (Cecchetti) or over the crown of the head (Russian).

first arabesque (Cecchetti)—Position in which the body is in profile to the audience. The supporting leg is the upstage leg. The forward arm is on the same side of the body as the supporting leg. The other arm opens to second position or slightly behind. The eyes focus straight ahead.

first arabesque (Russian)—The torso and downstage shoulder open from the bottom of the sternum. The forward arm is at shoulder height. The downstage arm is in second position or slightly behind.

first port de bras—Position in which the arms begin in fifth position en bas, or preparatory position. Both arms rise to first position, then open to second position. Both arms rotate, lifting the elbows slightly before floating downward and returning to starting position.

first position (arms)—The arms stretch in front of the body parallel to the bottom of the sternum or higher. The fingertips are slightly separated.

first position (feet)—The heels of the feet touch with both legs turned out equally.

FITT principle—Acronym for frequency, intensity, time, and type of activity performed.

flexing—See *foot flexion*.

flick and press—Exercise in which the foot flicks quickly from a full-foot position to a point off the floor. On the return path, the tips of the toes and the foot press with resistance through three-quarter relevé to the full-foot position.

Fokine, Michel (1880-1942)—Russian dancer and choreographer who joined Diaghilev's Ballets Russes. Fokine's ballets were central to the company's success from 1909 to 1912. His story ballets, such as *Firebird* and *Petrouchka*, established ballet as a dramatic form. In contrast, his signature work, *Les Sylphides*, was an abstract ballet in a romantic style.

Fontaine, Mlle La (1655-1738)—The first female professional ballet dancer. She appeared in *Le Triomphe de L'Amour* in 1681, performing in a floor-length court dress with high-heeled shoes.

foot flexion—Also called *flexing*; the reverse of pointing the foot. The flexion begins at the ankle joint with the heel pushing forward.

foot pedal—Exercise in which the action begins with a quick release from the ankle through the foot. The tips of the toes can point, resting either on the floor or just above it. On the return path, the tips of the toes and the foot press with resistance through three-quarter relevé to the full-foot position.

foot press—Exercise in which the foot stretches from the full-foot position to the three-quarter relevé position; the toes and metatarsals rest on the floor. On the return path, the foot resists as it presses to the full-foot position.

foot triangle—Three major points on the sole that come in contact with the floor.

fourth arabesque (Cecchetti)—The body faces a downstage corner most often. The downstage leg is the supporting leg similar to second arabesque, but in a demi-plié. The arms are the same as for first arabesque. The eyes focus to the downstage corner.

fourth arabesque (Russian)—The legs are in the same position as for third arabesque. The torso turns upstage, with the downstage arm stretching forward and the upstage arm extending behind. The arms create a continuous line through the body. The head looks toward the audience and tilts toward the downstage shoulder.

fourth position (arms)—One arm is rounded and high overhead and the other arm is curved in front of the waist. The arm in front is opposite to the foot in front in a fourth position.

fourth position (feet)—One foot is forward of the other foot. The distance between the back and the front foot is the length of one foot. For the beginning dancer, fourth position can be forward of either first position or third position.

fourth position en avant—In fourth position, one arm curves in front at the waistline and the other arm stretches in second position. The curved arm is opposite to the foot in front.

full-foot position—When the entire sole of the foot rests on the floor.

galliard—A lively triple-time couple dance with hops, jumps, and kicks; the second dance in the two-part suite.

gigue—A popular 16th- and 17th-century dance in triple time featuring fast footwork and performed in many versions. The final dance of the four-part suite.

glissade [glee-SAHD]—Gliding step that can be performed with or without change of feet to the side, its basic form.

Grahn, Lucille (1819-1907)—Danced the title role in *La Sylphide* in Denmark before dancing at the Paris Opéra, in other European capitals, and in Russia. Returning to Denmark, she became known as the Danish Taglioni.

grand allegro—Steps in the center moving across the floor; they include large jumps and leaps.

grand battement [grahn bat-MAHN]—Large beating, or kicking action of the leg into the air.

grand jeté [grahn zhuh-TAY]—Big leap; a large leap in which the body travels in an overcurve.

grand pas de deux—Performed by the ballerina and the premier danseur, it is the dance that showcases each dancer's ballet technique and artistry as dancers in the leading roles in the ballet.

grand plié [grahn plee-AY]—Large bend of the knees.

Grisi, Carlotta (1819-1899)—Italian dancer. She danced the lead role in the ballet *Giselle*, created by Jean Coralli and Jules Perrot with the scenario written by Théophile Gautier. Grisi became one of the most prominent ballerinas in the romantic era in European capitals and Russia. Many believe she was the first ballerina to wear a blocked slipper that enabled her to dance on pointe.

haut (high) dances—Court dances from the 15th and 16th centuries that featured springing, jumping, and kicking movements.

hyperextension—Condition that occurs because as the knees press backward, ligaments behind the knees permanently stretch.

Ivanov, Lev (1834-1901)—Russian dancer and choreographer at the Maryinsky Theatre. Ivanov choreographed *The Nutcracker*. His legacy is *Swan Lake* (second and fourth acts).

jeté [zhuh-TAY]—Thrown. Jump in which the back foot brushes full-foot to à la seconde and the body is pushed directly upward into the air. Both legs extend in a small second position before descending and landing with the front foot in demi-plié and the back foot in coupé derrière.

kinesthetic sense—Muscle, bone, and joint sense; being able to feel the body in space.

King, Alonzo—A native of Georgia. He trained in New York and performed with Dance Theatre of Harlem before establishing his company, LINES, in San Francisco in 1982. King has created contemporary ballets performed internationally by companies and on TV and film.

Kirkland, Gelsey (1952–)—Ballerina. She performed in many Balanchine and Robbins roles. From 1974 to 1984, she danced with American Ballet Theatre, partnering with Mikhail Baryshnikov.

knock-knees—When standing with the feet in parallel first position, the insides of the knees bow inward so that they touch. Scientific name is genu valgum.

Le Ballet-Comique de la Reine—A ballet work that was produced at the French court in 1581 and is considered the first ballet.

Lee, Mary Ann (1823-1899)—The first American Giselle. She trained in Philadelphia with Augusta Maywood. Lee performed in Europe, then she and her partner, George Washington Smith, formed a small American ballet troupe and toured cities as far west as St. Louis.

Legnani, Pierina (1863-1923)—Italian dancer who performed at the Maryinsky Theatre. As the Swan Queen, she executed 32 fouettés en tournant (whipping, continuous turns). She became an inspiration for Russian dancers to emulate her technical feats, and her work created a new standard for the ballerina in the classical era.

lift—See pull-up.

Louis XIV (1638-1715)—King of France. A dancer, producer of more than 1,000 ballets, and patron of the arts.

Lully, Jean Baptiste (1632-1687)—Italian musician and composer. He was King Louis XIV's supervisor of ballets.

Markarova, Natalia (1940–)—Graduate of the Vaganova Ballet Academy. She joined the Kirov Ballet dancing leading roles in classical ballets. In 1971, she defected to the United States and joined American Ballet Theatre. Her performances spanned from classical to contemporary ballets. She has revived and staged many classical and 20th-century ballets for companies around the world.

marking—Using small movements to indicate leg and arm movements of an exercise or combination.

Massine, Léonide (1896-1979)—Dancer and choreographer. He studied at the Imperial Ballet School and joined Diaghilev's Ballets Russes in 1913. He became the company's chief choreographer. His work Parade (1917) established him as a choreographer. In the 1930s Massine became director of the Ballet Russe de Monte Carlo. During his career he choreographed more than 100 ballets in two styles: story ballets with comic elements and abstract ballets performed to symphonic works.

Maywood, Augusta (1825-1870)—The first American ballerina. She made her debut in Philadelphia but spent much of her professional career in Europe, becoming a prima ballerina at La Scala in Milan. She appeared in New York in the Americanized version of La Sylphide titled The Mountain Sylph.

minuet—A complicated couple dance that displayed elegance of movement and manners in the ballroom that were required by 18th-century society.

Mitchell, Arthur (1934–)—First African American principal dancer with the New York City Ballet. He left the company to return to Harlem in 1968. Mitchell had starred in some of the seminal Balanchine works such as Agon. In 1969, Mitchell founded the Dance Theatre of Harlem featuring works by Balanchine, revised classics, and contemporary choreography.

movement principles—Incorporate scientific and aesthetic concepts into ballet technique.

musicality—Understanding of music; in dance, how execution of movement relates to the music.

Nijinsky, Vaslav (1890-1950)—A graduate of the Imperial Ballet School. He joined the Diaghilev Ballet as a dancer and became the company's choreographer after Fokine's departure in 1912. Nijinsky created L'Après-midi d'un Faune (Afternoon of a Faun) in 1912, Le Sacre du Printemps (The Rite of Spring) in 1913, and other avant-garde works. By 1917, Nijinsky became mentally ill and left the company. He spent the remainder of his life in a mental institution.

Noverre, Jean Georges (1727-1810)—Ballet master at the Paris Opéra and prolific choreographer. He is credited with creating more than 150 ballets. His lasting contribution was his Lettres sur la Danse et sur les Ballets (1760), which he penned to distinguish ballet as an art form distinct from opera and to state four principles as the foundation of ballets d'action.

Nureyev, Rudolf (1938-1993)—A star in the Soviet Union with the Kirov Ballet. He began his Western career when he defected to the United States in 1961 while on tour. In the United States he danced and choreographed or restaged ballets with major ballet and modern dance companies. In 1983 he became the director of the Paris Opera Ballet. Nureyev is considered one of the foremost male dancers of the 20th century.

opéra-ballets—Themed evening-long entertainments of the 18th century that included a series of opera and dance scenes.

overload principle—The body needs greater than normal stress, or load, to become stronger. After a period of time the body adapts to this stress, and greater stress will need to be added for further gains.

pas de Basque [pah duh bask]—Step of the Basque. This step is generally learned in a smooth, gliding adagio style. Later it can be executed with tiny jumps in a petit allegro style.

pas de bourrée [pah duh boo-RAY]—Step of the bourrée, or stuffed step, has the same name as a historical dance performed in the baroque period.

pas de chat [pah duh shah]—Step of the cat. Starting in demi-plié in third or fifth position, the back leg lifts to retiré derrière as the front foot pushes into the air. The front leg lifts to retiré devant during the air moment and then both feet land sequentially into demi-plié in third or fifth position.

pas de deux—Dance for two; challenges the male and female lead dancers' technique, virtuosity, and style. The highlight of the classical ballet was the grand pas de deux danced by the ballerina and the premier danseur.

passé [pa-SAY]—Passing step; the passé step learned at the barre is often performed as a series moving en arrière (backward), then en avant (forward).

pavane—A slow, stately processional dance in 4/4 time; the first dance in the two-part suite.

Pavlova, Anna (1881-1931)—Russian dancer and prima ballerina at the Maryinsky Ballet. She danced in Europe and appeared briefly with the Diaghilev Ballets Russes in its first season. In 1911 she formed her own company and toured throughout the world performing to audiences who had never before seen a ballet. Her repertoire included the classics and her experimental dances.

performance attitude—Thinking, acting, and moving like a dancer.

Perrot, Jules (1810-1892)—French dancer who studied with August Vestris. He danced as a soloist in London before returning to the Paris Opéra as Taglioni's partner and then teacher and partner with Carlotta Grisi. Perrot is considered the greatest male dancer of the romantic era. As a choreographer and ballet master in London, he applied the theories of Noverre in his romantic ballets. In contrast, his *Pas de Quatre* was a ballet that presented the four leading romantic ballerinas and their dancing styles. During the 1850s Perrot became the ballet master in St. Petersburg's Imperial Theatre, where he restaged his ballets and created new works.

personal space—Accommodates leg, arm, and body extensions without invading your neighbor's space while standing in one place or moving around the space.

Petipa, Marius (1819-1910)—French dancer, choreographer, and architect of classical ballet in Russia. Petipa created more than 50 ballets during his career at the Imperial Theatre. Some of his classic works have survived, such as *The Sleeping Beauty* (1890), the pas de deux from *Don Quixote* (1869), and *Swan Lake* (with Lev Ivanov, 1895). His lavish ballet productions extended to evening-long entertainments featuring ballet, mime, and character dances.

petit allegro [puh-TEE ah-LAY-groh]—The small, quick steps in this category use hops, leaps, and jumps that move from one foot to the other.

petit battement piqué [puh-TEE bat-MAHN pee-KAY]—Also called *battement tendu jeté pointe*; a stretched beating, thrown and pointed.

petit battement sur le cou-de-pied [puh-TEE bat-MAHN sewr luh koo-duh-PYAY]—Small beating at the neck of the foot.

piqué en avant [pee-KAY ahn a-VAHN]—Pricked step forward. The working leg begins pointe tendue devant. As the supporting leg executes a demi-plié, the working leg lifts to the height of a battement dégagé. The back leg pushes the weight quickly on to the front foot in three-quarter relevé. On relevé, the back heel touches behind the knee. Then the back foot steps into demi-plié directly behind the foot, which releases the front leg and foot into a battement dégagé.

pointe tendue—Stretched point.

pointing—Refers to the characteristic ballet foot position. It begins with flexing the ankle of the foot, then stretching and lifting the arch and the entire foot, continuing the extension through the lower foot, metatarsals, and toes.

port de bras [pawr duh brah]—Carriage of the arms; uses the entire arm and hand as a unit to move to and through a position. Port de bras can be simply moving your arms through a position when performing an exercise. Before each exercise and combination dancers perform port de bras, which serves as an introduction to performance.

port de corps [pawr duh kawr]—Carriage of the body; as part of the ballet barre the term refers to bending the torso forward, side, or back.

pre-barre exercises—Exercises that warm up body parts, increase flexibility and articulation, and help the dancer acquire the right mindset and breathing for the barre exercises that follow.

premier danseur—Leading male ballet dancer who performs solos, duets, or pas de deux and mimes the dramatic action of the ballet.

preparatory position—Starting position for port de bras in which arms are low; similar to fifth position en bas. The arms stretch downward and are slightly rounded in front of the body. There is space between the hands, and the sides of the little fingers do not touch the body.

PRICED—Protection, rest, ice, compression, elevation, and diagnosis; aids in recovery from minor injuries.

pull-up—Stretching the legs upward from the floor while engaging the abdominals and extending upward to lengthen the torso between the hips to the ribs. Also known as *lift*.

raked stage—An inclined stage, popular in the 18th century. This stage was higher at the back of the stage and lower in the front, nearest the audience.

regisseur—Individual who stages a dance work.

relevé [ruhl-VAY]—Raised; the heel of the foot lifts off the floor and the ball of the foot and the toes remain on the floor.

retiré [ruh-tee-RAY]—Withdrawn; the working foot moves through sur le cou-de-pied and traces a line up either the front or back of the supporting leg to rest under the kneecap, behind the knee, or at the side of the knee.

révérence [ray-vay-RAHNS]—A combination performed at the end of class to thank the teacher and accompanist. It involves port de bras with a bow for men and a curtsy for women.

Robbins, Jerome (1918-1998)—Dancer and choreographer who created works for the New York City Ballet and Broadway blockbusters such as *West Side Story* and *Fiddler on the Roof*.

romantic ballets—Dramatic action stories told through dancing, music, and pantomime in two acts. The romantic ballet era began in the

1830s and only lasted a few years, but its style and influence extended throughout the 19th century.

rond de jambe à terre [rawn duh zhahmb ah tehr]—Circular movement of the leg described by the pointed foot on the floor. The circular movement describes a half circle in two directions, en dehors (outside; away from the supporting leg) or en dedans (inside; toward the supporting leg).

Salle, Marie (1707-1756)—Known for her expressive style of dancing. She was one of the earliest recognized female choreographers. In the ballet *Pygmalion* (1734), Salle abandoned her tight bodice dress with pannier (large hooped skirt) for a simple muslin dress. She created further scandal by removing her wig and wearing her hair down.

sarabande—Originally from Spain, a lively solo dance in 3/4 time that became a sedate processional dance in the French court; the third dance of the four-part suite.

sauté [soh-TAY]—Jump.

second arabesque (Cecchetti)—Position in which the body is in profile to the audience. The upstage supporting leg is straight and turned out. The body line is square yet open to the audience. The forward arm is on the same side of the body as the leg extends behind. The other arm extends behind second position. The two arms create a complete diagonal line. The eyes focus over the fingertips of the forward hand, and the head tilts toward the audience.

second arabesque (Russian)—Similar to Russian first arabesque, the body is in profile with the supporting leg upstage from the audience. The downstage arm stretches forward while the upstage arm extends behind the body. The head turns to the audience.

second port de bras—The arms begin in fifth position en bas. Both arms rise to fifth position en haut. Then, the arms rotate to second position. The elbows lift slightly and the arms float downward, finishing fifth position en bas.

second position (arms)—Arms are immediately in front of the side of the body. Arms stretch from shoulder level or sloping downward and are slightly rounded.

second position (feet)—Feet separate the distance of one and one-half foot lengths up to shoulder width. Both great toes are on a straight line to ensure equal turnout of the legs.

Smith, George Washington (1820-1899)—Dancer and ballet master. He joined Fanny Elssler's company for its U.S. tour. He was the first American dancer to perform the role of Albrecht in *Giselle*.

sous-sus—Literally means under-over. A relevé, or rise, with the feet in a tight fifth position.

squareness—The shoulders and hips are parallel and on the same plane. Using the squareness principle, the dancer can focus on leg movements and their directions or on entire body movements in relation to the dance space.

stage directions—Relate to the performer standing on stage facing the audience. These stage areas include downstage toward the audience, upstage away from the audience, stage right to the right of the performer, and stage left to the left of the performer.

stance—How a dancer stands; the weight on both feet should be equally distributed over the foot triangle.

supporting foot—The one that supports the body weight.

sur la place—Staying in one place during a movement sequence that moves up or down within the space.

sur le cou-de-pied [sewr luh koo-duh-PYAY]—On the neck of the foot. In this position, the heel of the working foot rests on the front of the ankle and may or may not touch the back of the ankle. The toes and metatarsals may rest on the floor in a flexed position, or the foot might be pointed or flexed.

Taglioni, Marie (1804-1884)—Embodied the ethereal side of romanticism. Her role as the sylph in the *La Sylphide* (1832) made her a star. Her white costume and satin slippers became the model for the romantic tutu. In performance, her delicate movement, floating quality, and ability to pose for an instant on the tips of her toes (sur les pointes) captured the romantic spirit.

technique—Includes not only correct performance but also incorporation of movement principles that apply to the exercise or the step in a combination.

temps levé [tahm luh-VAY]—Time raised; a step that begins from two feet in third or fifth position and ends on one leg with the working foot touching the supporting leg either in front or back below the knee.

third arabesque (Cecchetti)—Position in which the body is in profile to the audience. The supporting leg is straight and turned out. Shoulders and hips are square. Both arms are forward; the upper arm is away from the audience and extends level to the top of the forehead. The lower arm is nearest the audience and at shoulder height. The eyes focus straight ahead as if looking through a window created by the arms.

third arabesque (Russian)—Position in which the body faces a downstage corner. The downstage leg is the supporting leg and is in demi-plié. The upstage leg stretches behind in croisé derrière. The upstage arm extends forward, while the other arm opens in second position. The face looks toward the forward hand.

third position (arms)—One arm is high overhead, while the other stretches in second position. If the right foot is front in third position, then the right arm is overhead.

third position (feet)—The heel of the front foot touches the middle of the arch of the back foot.

three-step turn—A small turning step practiced in preparation for other turning steps, such as chaînés.

tonnelet—An above-the-knee hooped skirt worn by male dancers in the first part of the 18th century.

turnout—A significant feature of ballet technique in which the legs outwardly rotate from the hip socket.

tutu—The ballerina's costume for classical ballet, featuring a tight bodice and multilayered skirt that varied in length from midcalf to above the knees to show the female dancer's technique and pointe work.

Vaganova, Agrippina (1879-1951)—A Russian ballerina and renowned teacher who formulated the Vaganova method used worldwide today.

Vestris, Auguste (1760-1842)—Son of Gaetan. He ruled the Paris Opéra stage in danseur noble roles during the 18th century.

Vestris, Gaetan (1729-1808)—The 18th-century leading danseur noble at the French Opéra who took the title God of the Dance.

weight distribution—The weight of the body on both feet or one foot.

weight transfer—Moving weight to the same foot, other foot, or both feet when standing or moving.

working foot—The foot that points in various directions on the floor, in the air, or resting on the supporting leg.

Zucchi, Virginia (1847-1930)—Italian dancer who performed with the St. Petersburg Ballet Theatre. She was a technical virtuoso with superb acting skills.

References
and Resources

Clippinger, Karen. 2007. *Dance anatomy and kinesiology*. Champaign, IL: Human Kinetics.

Corbin, Charles B., and Lindsey, Ruth. 2005. *Fitness for life*, 5th ed. Champaign, IL: Human Kinetics.

Cuypers, Koenraad. 2011. *Good Housekeeping,* November. http://besteducationpossible.blogspot.com/2011/10/tickets-to-health-and-happiness.html.

Grant, Gail. 1961. *Technical manual and dictionary of classical ballet*. New York: Kamin Dance.

Haas, Jacqui Greene. 2010. *Dance anatomy*. Champaign, IL: Human Kinetics.

Human Kinetics. 2010. *Health and wellness for life*. Champaign, IL: Author.

International Association for Dance Medicine and Science. 2011. Dance fitness. www.iadms.org.

Kassing, Gayle. 1999. *Interactive beginning ballet technique* [CD-ROM]. Champaign, IL: Human Kinetics.

Kassing, Gayle. 2007. *History of dance: An interactive arts approach*. Champaign, IL: Human Kinetics.

Kassing, Gayle, and Jay, Danielle. 1998. *Teaching beginning ballet technique*. Champaign, IL: Human Kinetics.

Kassing, Gayle, and Jay, Danielle. 2003. *Dance teaching methods and curriculum design*. Champaign, IL: Human Kinetics.

Vaganova, Agrippina. 1965. *Basic principles of classical ballet: Russian ballet technique,* 2nd ed. London: Adam & Black.

Index

Note: The letters *f* and *t* after page numbers indicate figures and tables, respectively.